EMPOWER THEN LEAD

EMPOWER THEN LEAD

Have a Greater Impact by Setting Up Your
Team for Success

Matt Blakely

Advanced Reader's Copy

Published January 19, 2018

ISBN: 1984026909

ISBN 13: 978-1984026903

Further changes may be made before the final version is published.

CONTENTS

PART 2: LEAD

INTRODUCTION

I'll never forget a guy I used to see at the gym many years ago. He carried himself with more confidence than anyone else I'd ever seen around the weights, but his physique didn't exactly match his demeanor. I'd put him at about twenty years old, five-and-a-half feet tall, and maybe 140 pounds. Maybe.

My friend and I, who were much younger and more immature back then, used to call him Captain Tank, based solely on the fact that he only wore tank tops. We also thought the nickname was ironic since he wasn't exactly built like a tank.

Captain Tank's routine was always the same. You could predict every move. He would do a set with free weights and then throw the dumbbells to the ground as if they were on fire. Then he'd let out the strangest sound, like someone yelling the word "yeah" blended with a loud grunt. (It might be easier to imagine if you try to make the sound yourself.) His face had a stern look of determination, almost bordering on anger. He would rapidly pace back and forth in front of the mirror to psych himself up while approvingly nodding his head, still with a look of intensity.

I think you get the picture. He might as well have jumped out of the pages of a comic book with his superhero persona. I think I even saw him kiss his flexed bicep a couple of times during the pacing phase, although my buddy thinks I'm embellishing that part to make the memory better.

But surprisingly, all of that wasn't what was most memorable to me. What really stood out was not just this post-set celebration ritual, but the fact that he had absolutely no idea how to lift weights; not a blessed clue. He would do dumbbell bicep curls with such a swinging motion that sheer momentum alone would bring the weights up to his chest.

So to clarify, he was trying to do an exercise to work a muscle without using said muscle. That's like saying you want to learn Spanish and then moving to France. Somehow he continued in the gym like this for months while his form, and consequently his physique, never improved.

I haven't seen Captain Tank in years, but I think of him often when I watch some business leaders in action. They work really hard and doing lots of *stuff*, but they're not doing what's needed to get them where they want to be, or to help them make the impact they had hoped for.

It's unfortunate when you break it down. In Captain Tank's case, he wasn't going to have big biceps because he wasn't doing the right things to produce those results. And the same thing can happen to you or I.

VISION BINDERS

A friend recently told me a story similar to Captain Tank's (without the biceps part). He owns a business and is very successful, as far as I can tell. I mean, every suit I've seen him wear probably costs more than all of my suits combined.

When we got together, he shared with me how busy he was. He wanted to grow his business, but for some reason he couldn't. Even with a small team working for him, he still worked long hours and could never seem to catch a break.

I noticed that his office had stacks of handwritten papers that he had crammed into folders. He called them vision binders. They contained all the business plans he'd formulated a couple of years earlier while on a rare beach vacation. But they now sat on a shelf, collecting dust, while the hectic day-to-day routine persisted with little growth or advancement. I wondered about the incredible ideas that might have been wasting away in those pages.

He told me that his ultimate goal seemed unachievable: freedom to build his business while not being bogged down by the day-to-day tasks. He wanted less direct involvement, and more time to focus on vision, expansion, and growth.

Here's the problem though: Similar to Captain Tank, my friend wasn't doing the things that would get him where he wanted to be. He looked across his desk at me, frustrated with his situation, and envied what I had. Which is funny, because I was in the same situation only two years earlier.

SUCKED BACK IN

For the first ten years as an entrepreneur, I wasn't at all a *leader* as I have now come to see it. I was maybe a decent manager and certainly good at doing some stuff, but I wasn't a good leader.

I originally started a software company because I was good at making software. That was the first strike against me; I learned that it can be a challenge to be a leader when you're too good at something specific. It can be quite difficult to go from doing something you're good at, supported by years of education and experience, to a leadership role that you know very little about. Since I was used to building software, I not only worked to create products, but I micromanaged the team and was always in the middle of things.

As the years went on, I became frustrated. I was always extremely busy and couldn't get control of my time. I remember being nervous that the world might fall apart if I took a vacation, which would almost ruin the time away anyway. I would check in at least daily and always be available should something go awry. It almost seemed as if I were chained to my computer.

I would often wonder why other people on my team didn't come up with the ideas that I thought of or couldn't do the things I could do. I came to believe that I was the only one who could do great work. You know the silly expression: "If you want something done right, do it yourself." Really it should be "If you want to keep doing the same thing yourself over and over again forevermore, do it yourself," but I guess that's not as catchy.

I continued to persevere with brute force, as if one day I would magically emerge from the haze as a prominent and influential leader with a wildly successful business. But just like my expensively suited friend and Captain Tank, I wasn't doing the right things to produce the results I wanted.

My actions didn't affect only me negatively; they left my team unhappy and less engaged in the company. For them, work just paid the bills. They were not not passionate about it. The culture was bad, and team morale was low. Many people left the company entirely, leaving me to work harder and run more of the show.

In addition to these issues, what annoyed me most was the lack of business growth. I attempted to expand and branch out a couple of times, trying to pursue some pages out of my own "vision binders." I had a document called "Initiatives" that I was very excited about when I wrote it. But without fail, I would get sucked back into the day-to-day with client issues or product-support concerns, and I'd put the growth and expansion plans back on the shelf once again.

The way I see it, there is an upper limit to the potential of leaders who are directly involved in everything around them. It's basic math. If I have my hands in every detail of the company, I might be able to micromanage a handful of people, but at some point, I will run out of hours in a day. My limitations will cap the company's potential.

People often say they are juggling too many balls. It's a silly cliché, but it's a decent way to describe the problem. The juggler can't take a break because everything will fall to the ground. And he can't take on more balls because he can only juggle so many. Likewise, business leaders who try to do everything will remain stuck, and eventually that will catch up with them.

MULTIPLIED IMPACT

I hate to admit it, but for years I saw people as a means to my personal advancement. I desperately wanted to have more influence and to make a greater impact, even though I see now that I had no clue what "impact" even meant. I didn't realize that doing the right things for my business included a significant investment in the people around me . . . the very people I didn't value.

My big discovery was that I could multiply my impact by empowering others. I don't mean the kind of empowering that is so often thrown around as a buzzword. I'm talking about handing over real power to people—real responsibility to make decisions, not only piecemeal tasks. I found out that my impact as a leader is multiplied through an empowered team. That's how exponential growth can happen and a business can scale.

AN ALTERNATE UNIVERSE

There's just one little catch. You'll probably have to drop many preconceived notions of what you think a leader does to realize this multiplication. Most people think of leaders as being in the spotlight, running the show, and being the heroes. But that notion has to be flipped upside down to see the most dramatic results. True leaders make their teams the heroes. They invest in others, setting their teams up for far greater success than they could achieve on their own.

In this alternate universe, you obsess over how you can help your team to constantly improve, rather than preparing a report or responding to a client. If your job involves hundreds of emails, a full task list, or a packed calendar of events, your team is in trouble. You will remain the busy hero, but there will be a cost.

I see many leaders trying to be the heroes all the time, often with decent intentions, and it's hard to watch. They are burned out, their teams are deflated, and their organizations aren't growing. Nevertheless, they cling to their control and position, doing the same things over and over with the same results.

There is a huge contradiction, however, when you flip the org chart upside down and serve your team in a more supportive role. You might think that setting others up for success will bring you down, but you'll actually rise in influence. Being a supportive leader isn't a demotion; it's an incredible win-win for you, the team, and the organization.

BIGGER THAN YOURSELF

Let me tell you how things ended up for me. Despite being in a complex industry, and despite my efforts to do everything myself, I was eventually able to escape the details. I never dreamed that would be possible. These changes I made allowed me to disconnect, and things ran smoothly without my constant intervention. The company was positioned for growth for the first time, and that's exactly what happened. In fact, the year this new framework was implemented, we saw revenue triple.

Although these outcomes were amazing, they are not what motivated me to write this book. The real transformation inside me is what I want to share with you.

It might sound a little sappy, but I've come to care about the positive impact on the people around me more than anything. I saw a radical transformation in the company culture. People wanted to be at the office.

They were thriving and doing amazing work. Potential was being unlocked that I never thought possible.

After that experience, I now want to see leaders fulfilled in their roles and to see the people they lead thriving under great leadership. When leaders improve and focus outward, everyone wins.

When I refer to leaders, I'm not just talking about CEOs. For me, a leader is anyone who oversees people: a manager, a teacher, a parent, a pastor, a coach, and so on.

I have a neon sign in my office that says, "Much Is Required." Leaders' actions have a significant impact on the people they lead. That influence is a tremendous responsibility. When a leader invests in others, many people benefit: the leaders, their teams, the families of the team members, and beyond. That thought affects everything I do. That's why I believe in empowerment so much—the positive impact on people.

You have to decide whether you want to build something bigger than yourself that brings out the best in everyone around you. If so, then your full-time job becomes setting other people up for success. The other option is to haphazardly swing the dumbbells around every day while practically breaking your back. The choice is yours.

This book summarizes what I've learned about empowering people and leading effectively and the phenomenal results that took place. And because I'm a recovering control freak, I especially speak to the mindset changes that must take place for long-term results.

The book is divided in two sections: "Empower" and "Lead." Before we can even learn how to lead, the foundation of a fully empowered team needs to be in place. And that's where we're starting.

Oh, and to answer your question about Captain Tank, I'm sorry to admit that I never took the time to help the poor guy. I hadn't discovered others-focused leadership quite yet.

SUMMARY

· Many leaders work hard and are extremely busy, but they are not seeing the growth and impact they want.

· Many people are promoted to a position of leadership based on subject-matter expertise, but they lack training on how to lead.

· The day-to-day of many leaders often consists of direct involvement in the details, instead of doing the things that facilitate long-term, sustained growth.

· There is a limit to the potential of leaders who are directly involved in everything and with everyone around them.

· You need to look in the mirror and see if you could be the cause for limiting your impact.

· Leaders should focus on setting up others for success; in turn their influence will rise, and their impact will be greater.

· Real impact is made by empowering others (empower) and then by playing a supporting role (lead).

- There is great responsibility that comes with leading people.
- When leaders improve and focus outwards, everyone wins.

Ask Yourself: What is my desired impact and what is in the way? What percentage of the problem is caused by me?

PART ONE

EMPOWER

- ONE -

CONTROL VERSUS EMPOWERMENT

I learned a lot about what control looks like from a kids' soccer coach. My oldest son's team was playing a team whose coach perfectly illustrated the opposite of empowerment. I use the term "playing" loosely, because six-year-old kids really don't play a game of soccer; they chase each other around the field and occasionally kick the ball in the right direction, by accident. But back to the coach.

Have you ever been at a kids' sporting event that someone took way too seriously? I think this guy, who I'll call Coach, thought his team was in the World Cup. (I'm pretending I know anything about sports.) In his mind, his self-worth and livelihood were based on the outcome of this forty-five-minute game. Meanwhile, most of the parents were checking their phones or shooting the breeze with other parents, just having a relaxing Thursday evening in suburbia.

Coach's intensity was okay, I guess, if you're that type of guy. But the way he went about trying to secure the victory was painful to watch. His coaching MO was based on two approaches: yelling and moving.

Yelling was plan A. He would holler at the kids, telling them specifically where to stand and what to do. "Jackson! Go stand next to Chase, and don't let the ball get by you!" Or, "Peter, you're a goalie—stand in front of the net instead of behind it!" But plan A rarely met his rigid standards; therefore, plan B inevitably followed.

The best way I can explain plan B is to compare it with playing chess. To make a move, a player picks up a chess piece, such as a pawn, and moves it to a specific spot. That's exactly what Coach did with his players.

In these games, coaches were allowed to go on the field with the kids, and let me tell you, Coach took full advantage of that option. The chessboard was the soccer field, and the chess pieces were the six-year-old players. He would grab a "pawn" and literally move him by the head to the exact location where he presumed the play of the century would take place.

Remember that the kids were six years old. Not seven. Not ten. Six. They were in grade one. They were just learning how to read short words like "cat" or "dad," and to count to one hundred. They simply wanted to run around and have fun with their friends. And really they came for the treat at the end of the game. I'm a firm believer in challenging kids and helping them grow, but something about Coach's approach didn't seem right to me.

Do you think the kids understood why they were forcefully moved to one spot from another spot three feet away? Would they know where to stand next time? Did they ever get to suggest plays or ideas? And wouldn't treating them this way cause them turn off their brains, or even cause them to despise the game and never want to play again?

The bottom line is that Coach was telling the kids exactly what to do, even though they didn't understand and weren't allowed to make decisions on their own. Those kids weren't being set up to become great soccer players—they were simply pawns in someone else's game. And that's what controlling leaders do to their own teams.

(Despite Coach trying to disqualify the winning goal on a technicality, let the record state that my son's team won. But who's counting, right?)

ELUSIVE CREATURES

When I tell this story about Coach, people usually say something like, "Oh man, I can't believe someone would actually do that—what an idiot!" Or they say, "Dude, my friend works for a boss just like that!" It's funny, though, how everyone you talk to seems to know a controlling leader, but you never actually meet one in person.

Here's an experiment for you to try. If you're talking to a group of people, ask how many have met really controlling leaders. You'll probably see most hands go up (except poor sports like me who are concerned about being controlled). Then ask how many people consider themselves to be controlling leaders, and watch 100 percent of the hands immediately come down. You might be tempted to think this is a coincidence. But maybe something else is going on.

I want to caution you against writing this control thing off as being a message only for *other* leaders. I don't know how to say this nicely, so I'll go ahead and give it to you straight. We've been together long enough to be real with each other, right?

It's *you* too. That's right—*you*. The one with the skeptical look on your face, looking down at the page.

I know the soccer story is an extreme example of controlling leadership, but it's important to note that control happens in degrees. You can't just check yes or no on a survey to answer the question of whether you are a controlling leader. It's not black-and-white. You might be naturally controlling in subtle ways that you don't even realize, even though you might look down on similar behavior in other people.

KNOWLEDGE IS POWER

We've already established that controlling leaders tell people exactly what to do when they don't really understand and aren't allowed to make decisions on their own. But let's go a little deeper. Control attempts to directly affect someone's behavior, almost like reducing someone's free will. It's taking away a person's option to make a good, informed decision. This can be done in two ways: by withholding the option to make decisions or by withholding information.

The most obvious way to control someone is to make all the decisions yourself and then tell people what to do. This is like Coach coming up with the next play and physically moving people to the right spots. In this scenario, your team just executes the tasks they're told to do. You, as the one in charge, make all the decisions and have all the responsibility and ownership. There's limited space for feedback, opinions, or ideas from your team.

The less obvious way to control someone is to withhold information that would help someone make good decisions. This is like Coach not explaining why a play was chosen or what a good play even looks like. People really can't make good decisions if they don't know enough to understand what is going on. To build on the expression, "Knowledge is power," holding back knowledge means holding back power.

PLAYBOOK OF A CONTROL FREAK

Let me give you a few examples of what control looks like in a workplace.

I'll start with *the task dictator*. Have you ever quickly dictated a task to someone on the run? You say, "Do this, then this, then call this person, and then fill out that paper." The person you're talking to is just a pawn, blindly executing your commands.

In these scenarios of drive-by delegation, it could be a big task that requires a lot of background information for the person to succeed. But in this approach you don't position the person to make decisions or to come up with ideas.

I've even heard guys dictating tasks at bathroom urinals. This is wrong on so many levels. Not to mention, how do you expect the poor guy to write it all down?

I used to send notes to people that said things such as, "Can you call Jim and tell him the status?" I was giving the steps, but there was no clarity about when I was expecting it to be done or what to do with the information. I left a lot open to interpretation.

Then there's *the classic micromanager.* You direct the completion of a task because you didn't provide clear expectations to the people assigned to the job. You check over people's shoulders as they progress through the steps. If you change your mind, you tell them to do it another way. You just drag the soccer players around by their heads.

One of my least favorite forms of micromanagement is when leaders create the illusion that people have real responsibility, when in fact they keep stealing it back. Maybe someone on your team appears to have ownership over a certain department, yet you end up leading their meetings and doing all the talking. This is *the microphone hog.* Your team doesn't have a chance to get a word or thought in. I used to dominate meetings, and did almost all the talking. People would literally look at me and pause before making a comment since they assumed I would speak first.

Maybe you even have meetings and make decisions about a subject that someone else is responsible for without inviting that person to contribute. This is *the backroom decider.* In my case, two or three of us would meet behind closed doors, protecting information as if we were part of a top-secret military mission. We would make decisions on behalf of other people. Meanwhile the person who was supposed to own the area was left out, confused, and annoyed. Let me be clear—when I did this, I stole their ownership.

I know some leaders who ask their team to copy them on every email they send to clients. This is a classic move by *the stalker*. There's nothing like scrutinizing everything a person writes to kill ownership and confidence. You might as well just stand over everyone's shoulders all day whispering, "Be very, very careful—I'm watching you."

Then, if you're copied on a response from a client, you quickly devise the perfect action plan before your team has any chance to think or act. Or worse, you write the email yourself and feed it to your team to send the response. (I confess; I've done this once or twice or fifty times before.) If this is you, stop now. I'm begging you. Your team either hates you for this or has given up thinking altogether since it's clear you're running the whole show.

Another way leaders exert control is what I call *the scatterbrained corrector*. Controlling forms of correction happen when the leader gets mad about something that wasn't clear in the first place. And it happens when leaders are inconsistent about the things they choose to correct.

Can you think back to a time when someone corrected you and you had absolutely no idea it was even a rule? It's quite deflating. You didn't have the information about what to do or not to do, and then you are reprimanded for a decision that you couldn't have possibly known was a bad one. It's really not fair. Yet this type of correction is all too common.

Looking back, my biggest issue with correcting people was wrongly believing that the expectations were obvious. I had an ideal in my head of how I wanted everyone to perform at work, but I never set people up to be able to achieve it. I believed that certain behaviors were implied. So I would constantly correct people, even doing so rudely in public settings. I'm sure people felt as if they couldn't do anything right. They knew I was annoyed with them, but they likely didn't know why.

There's so much more I can say, but for now, I want you to get a picture of the ways control can look. Do any of these scenarios seem familiar? Are you the classic micromanager, making sure everything gets done just the way you want? Maybe you creepily look over people's shoulders, like the stalker? Or you could be a combination of these types, depending on the moment of the day.

BUILDING TOWERS

After reading some of these examples, you may be feeling a little down on yourself, so let me try to make you feel a little better. My three-year-old son helped teach me that controlling tendencies may not be your fault.

The other day, he asked me to build a tower with him. I hate to brag, but I can build some unbelievable towers. I start with a sturdy base, obviously, and then I work from there to get it as high as possible. So when he asked me to help, I brought my A game.

We went to the playroom, he dumped out the blocks, and we went to work. First, he put a block down, and then I jumped in and placed a block in the perfect spot, since I knew just how critical the foundation was for success.

"I'll move it here," my son said as he took the block I'd just put down and moved it somewhere else. I was slightly deflated but I wondered if his selection could have been an accident. Perhaps he had reached for a piece from the pile but got mine instead. But after the next block, he repeated, "No, like this, Daddy." And again he moved the block to another spot.

This pattern continued one by one until I inevitably became a sore loser and said, "If you're not going to take any of my ideas, maybe you should just build the tower by yourself." I said it with a whiny tone that had a similar effect of saying, "I'm not going to invite you to my birthday party."

"No, you do it too, Daddy," he said, with a concerned tone that seemed more about my participation than my contribution.

"Okay, fine. How about we start with four blocks to make the bottom really strong? That cool, buddy?" I said, hopeful.

He paused before responding, "Maybe this way, Daddy." Then he continued doing it his way.

Here's my point: My three-year-old son didn't have years of bad work experiences. He hadn't taken courses on how to be a controlling manager. Somehow it was natural for him to tell other people exactly what to do. Control was natural.

The desire to control situations was ingrained in him at a young age. He naturally understood that if you want someone to do something, you either tell the person what to do, or you do it yourself. Kids already think that's what it means to be a boss or manager.

To be fair, I get why people are drawn to ordering others around. That seems like the fastest way to get what you want without having to rely on other people, and that's attractive.

But you're reading this because you presumably want something you don't have now: maybe time, business growth, more impact, or better performance from people. So, what is the alternative to control?

THE DRIVER'S SEAT

We've established that control takes away someone's option to make decisions. Leaders can do this by not sharing the power to make decisions or by withholding information people need to make good decisions. We may have established that you're guilty of these controlling tendencies, at least at some level, but that you come by it honestly. Now let's look at empowerment.

"Empowerment" is a word that's often misunderstood, but I'll do my best to clear it up. In its simplest form, empowerment is about giving power to others. It's exactly what control holds back: the power to understand and the power to make decisions. Control restricts power whereas empowerment shares it. Control forces people to carry out your decisions, while empowerment allows others to decide.

Thinking back to the soccer comparison, an empowered team looks a lot different from Coach's team. Empowered players would know what positions they're playing and why. They would not be told exactly where to stand. They would know to guard open players on the opposing team, without being dragged into position by the head. They would look for opportunities to pass the ball, to make a play up the field. (Of course we're dealing with six-year-olds here, so our expectations should be realistic.)

The goal of empowerment is to put your team in the driver's seat to make the decisions. They can obey the rules of the road, like watching the speed limit or stopping at a red light. They can also respond to unpredictable situations, such as a deer jumping onto the road.

Rather than waiting for you to direct, an empowered team comes up with ideas and takes initiative. They do this without needing you to be a backseat driver. (Notice I didn't say you wouldn't want to.) Does that sound like a world you want to live in?

Being a controlling manager is almost like being a backseat driver of many cars at the same time. You're on the phone with all the drivers, monitoring their positions and directing them. However, because all the decisions come from you, all the unforeseen problems are your responsibility. I hope the limitations of control are becoming more apparent.

JIMMY

The way some people order meals at fancy restaurants perfectly illustrates of the results of control (stay with me for a minute). I was recently out for dinner with a friend whose name and meal choice I will conceal to protect his or her identity.

The waitress walked up to the table and motioned to my friend Jimmy. "What can I get you?"

"What comes on the steak?" asked Jimmy, as if he were cross-examining a witness at a trial.

"It is coated in a blend of barbeque sauce and butter with a little . . ." Jimmy abruptly cut her off. He had heard enough.

"That won't work," he said, shaking his head disapprovingly. "What about the salmon? How is that prepared?"

At this point, I was slouching pretty low in my seat, almost off the chair. Meanwhile, the waitress was still nice and composed; clearly she had dealt with people like Jimmy before. "The salmon is baked to perfection with a coating of lime, cilantro, and . . ." She slowed a little at the end based on the disappointed look on Jimmy's face.

Jimmy capitalized on the delay and jumped right in. "Okay, how about this." The waitress touched her pen to her notepad to indicate that she was poised and ready for the dictation. "Give me the salmon, but make sure it's a little underdone. Tell the chef to squeeze half a lemon on it before putting it in the oven and then add cilantro after it comes out. I like my cilantro cool and fresh."

I'll spare you the rest of this story, but think how incredibly frustrating it must have been for the chef to take this dictation and follow the specific steps. Jimmy was about one step away from slapping on an apron, waltzing into the kitchen, and making the whole meal himself. He was a complete amateur telling a professional chef with years of training and experience how to cook. In fact, Jimmy was demanding only a fraction of what the chef was capable of delivering.

That's the first result of control—reduced potential. Control pushes away capable, intelligent, creative, high-performance people who want to understand and grow. Your team could possibly get by under this type of leadership in an extremely predictable, methodical industry. But for anything even slightly complex or creative, organizations need the best from people.

The idea with empowerment is to realize the full potential of your team so that they can offer their best efforts, skills, and ideas in a rapidly changing world. Empowerment allows the chef to use his or her strengths to create something incredible.

Let's say you're only getting an average of two-thirds of the potential from each person on your team (which is generous, from the stats I've seen). If you can get the remaining third, you're basically adding an extra person for every three people on the team. Think about your own team: What percentage of their potential do you think you are seeing now?

The second big issue with control is long-term dependency. When you're so involved in the details, your team gets used to taking out a pen and paper and writing down the instructions. But that's a very short-term mindset. You'll always be in the middle of the details and decisions, which can be tiring and frustrating. Like my expensively suited friend, you'll be forever working *in* the business but not *on* the business, and that's not scalable.

With empowerment, the team's dependency on you as a leader is removed. You are freed up and are no longer a bottleneck. In a sense, empowerment moves you from doing things in series to doing them in parallel. If you control the decisions, you reduce the range of possibilities. Think of the potential if those decisions could happen without you. Empowerment multiplies potential, giving you the choice of where to spend your time, whether it be growing the business, or working fewer hours.

Those two points—the potential of the team and the scalability of your organization—sum up the major differences between control and empowerment. These results solve the dilemma of how to make more impact in less time. It will be helpful to keep these benefits in mind for the rest of the book; they will motivate you by helping you see what you have to gain (or lose).

Let's move on to how empowerment works. The starting point for me, and for a lot of people, is about mindset. We have to have the right mindset before we can empower people.

SUMMARY

- Controlling leaders tell people exactly what to do when they don't understand why and aren't allowed to make decisions.

- Control can happen by not allowing people to make decisions or by withholding information needed to make good decisions.

- Control is often natural; it can seem instinctively easier to tell people what to do.

- Control happens in degrees; you might control in subtle ways that you don't realize.

- The degree to which you empower people is directly related to your impact.

- Examples of control:
  - The Task Dictator: Provide step-by-step instructions to be exactly followed.
  - The Classic Micromanager: Direct every aspect of completing a task.
  - The Microphone Hogger: Dominate the conversation, keeping the team quiet.
  - The Backroom Decider: Exclude the team from decisions made behind closed doors.

- The Stalker: Look over the shoulders of your team.

- The Scatterbrained Corrector: Correcting inconsistently, including about things that were never clear.

- Empowerment gives to other people the same power that is held back with control: the power to understand and the power to make decisions.

- Control pushes people to carry out your decisions whereas empowerment allows others to decide.

- With empowerment, the team exercises ownership and takes responsibility.

- Empowerment helps realize the potential of your team and allows business scalability.

Ask yourself: In what ways am I controlling? What results has this produced?

- TWO -

ASSUME SUCCESS

I'm going to put it right out there that I was controlling over the years because of one crippling thought: I didn't think other people could be as good as I was. I thought I was the only one who could do things right. I thought I would always make the best decisions, have the best ideas, and do the best work. I was skeptical about the potential of others. Instead of assuming people would succeed, I assumed they would fail.

If you can't relate and you think everyone is jam-packed with potential, just skip to the next chapter. But for everyone else, read on.

I was with a group of business owners a few months ago, and one older, successful member of the group was advising a younger guy on the topic of growing a business. The advice was essentially to stay small and not count on anyone to do anything well. He used a phrase that really stood out to me: "People are problems." And he wasn't the only person with that thought. Over half of the group gave approving nods as he said it, as if he had unlocked one of the universe's great secrets. In the eyes of most of the people in that group, everyone else in the world is pathetic.

PSYCHOLOGICAL ANALYSIS

We often control people because we're skeptical that they can measure up. Admitting that is a good start. But I want to know why. Why do we think that? Where does that mindset come from?

Let me just say that I'm underqualified to give a physiological or psychological analysis related to this question, so I will simply share what I've learned from my experience. I found that I held some assumptions that limited my mindset.

Assumptions are ideas you accept to be true without proof. Certain factors may have fueled your assumptions, but you don't have conclusive confirmation that they are true. Every day you make decisions based on a lot of assumptions—some right and some wrong.

Let's say you meet a man who seems unpleasant and who speaks in a monotone way with few facial expressions. You may have an assumption that a bland tone must mean a bad mood. But there could be many reasons for the tone. Maybe it just comes naturally, and the person is currently trying to improve it. Or it could be that he is trying to act more professional and hasn't figured out the right balance. And so on.

So, your assumption about this person could be wrong. But it would be hard to get the facts if you both weren't willing to have an honest conversation. It would be socially unacceptable to ask a complete stranger why he's so rude. Instead, you'd assume that the guy is a jerk and you'd probably get out of that conversation as soon as possible.

I have an incredibly frustrating issue where my hands frequently sweat. I looked it up online and found out there is a name for the condition: hyperhidrosis. The article I read said it is "a common disorder which produces a lot of unhappiness." Because of it (the condition, not the unhappiness), I try to avoid shaking hands. When I do this, one of two things happens: In scenario A, the person thinks I'm awkward or a jerk as I try to avoid such a common greeting; or in scenario B, the person forces a handshake and then thinks I'm nervous as they get a handful of hyperhidrosis, which they subtly (or not so subtly) wipe off.

It's sad that we have so many incorrect assumptions about people. Perhaps you made a bunch of less-than-ideal decisions today that were based on bad assumptions. That's a scary thought.

FUZZY DETAILS

I've read a lot recently about the origins of our assumptions. Thoughts such as "People are problems" don't just form out of nowhere.

Let's say you have an encounter with a lady on your team who doesn't do something you thought she would. Maybe one morning you ask her to prepare a sales report. Closer to the end of the day, you're concerned and follow up to check the status, since you haven't heard anything. Sound familiar? Turns out she is struggling to finalize the details, but you have her send it over to you as-is.

Now think about how you log this memory in your brain. You remember that she was slow, unreliable, and not thorough. You have trouble shaking off the feeling of annoyance. That's strike one for that person.

But then a similar thing happens again a couple weeks later. On the next report she forgets to include some key information—strike two. The issues continue until you see that person as being incompetent. Then, you subconsciously decide to only give her simple tasks, or ignore her altogether.

To make things worse, this same pattern happens with other people you work with. The details of exactly what happened are fuzzy, and your brain summarizes complicated events into a simple thought: Everyone around you fails, and no one has a clue what they're doing.

The belief that people always fail becomes the foundation of your assumptions about how people will perform in the future, and becomes the lens through which you see the world. This lens then affects every interaction you have with people. And when your default assumption is that people always fail, your default response will be control.

So, bad assumptions often come from bad experiences. But here's the issue: We don't usually reflect on the circumstances surrounding these experiences, especially in an unbiased way, before we accept our assumptions as facts. And that usually happens unintentionally.

But consider whether the experiences that form our assumptions about people are flawed. For example, what if a person wasn't the right fit for a role and would have performed better in a different area?

Or, perish the thought, what if the problem was you? What if you didn't set them up for a win? I simply want you to open your mind to that possibility. What if the situation wasn't as simple as someone just messing up?

Looking at the sales report example again, here's how you should have filed away the memory in an unbiased, truthful way. First, you'd analyze how you made the request for the report. Were you clear about exactly what you wanted and why you wanted it? Did you say exactly when it was due and why? Were you aware of her other priorities?

Then you'd look at the work itself. Did you ever share all the background information that was necessary to produce the report? Did you set her up to understand all aspects of the numbers? Was she the best person to ask for this? Did you ask her a single question during the whole exchange?

If you file away the answers to those questions, your memory of the events will be more complete and less biased. It's extremely misleading to summarize the memory as the person failing.

A SELF-FULFILLING PROPHECY

Let me tell you the condensed version of how my limiting assumption emerged.

1. I started a company for which I was doing most of the work myself (i.e. I built most of the product, spent months with the first client, etc.).
2. I handed off a lot of tasks but didn't properly set people up for success.

3. I disengaged from the company with a false sense of security that all was well.

4. I found out all was not well, formed an assumption that people could never be as good as me, and became a control freak.

5. I saw the light. (If only it didn't take me ten years to reach this point.)

I'm embarrassed to write this because the problem now seems so obvious. I failed to empower my team. I held all the power and created a self-fulfilling prophecy that I was the best. As a result, the company couldn't grow beyond my direct control.

My journey was like running a one-hundred-meter relay race. At the end of the first leg, at the exchange zone, I decide to throw the baton as far ahead as I can. I am relieved to be done with my part and am ready to relax. Meanwhile, my teammate runs ahead to catch the flying baton before it hits the ground. Then I hear the crowd erupt, only to find out my teammate drops the baton. From my vantage point, I assume my teammate is letting *me* down. Failing to see my own problems in this scenario, I begin to assume that my team isn't reliable.

For the next event, I decide I'm not going to pass the baton at all. I run the whole four-hundred meters myself. As a result, I'm exhausted by the end, and the other teams are far ahead of me. Despite the facts, I still go on thinking that I had made the best choice by running the race alone because I believe my teammates will only let me down.

Sounds pretty silly, right? Oh, and I can't forget to tell you how my story ends in this comparison. Someone eventually shows me a replay of the original race when I threw the baton and explains that throwing batons is a really dumb idea. I then have to choose whether to be embarrassed or to admit the error of my ways and get back in the race, so to speak.

If you have a similar skeptical mindset, maybe you can relate to this pattern.

BECOMING AN OPTIMIST

I have something important and difficult to ask of you. I want you to completely clear your past negative assumptions about people. In other words, I want you to assume your assumptions are failing you.

Before you object, ask yourself this question: Is your current way of thinking achieving the outcomes you want? If not, it might be worth trying a new way.

From the moment my kids were born, I looked at them with complete optimism. Even though they couldn't walk or talk at first, I truly believed they could do great things someday. I saw future leaders. I believed they could far surpass me. And I believe that those subconscious thoughts greatly affect how I view them and deal with them.

Imagine if you saw people on your team with such potential. How would that affect how you deal with them? What would you involve them in? If you treated people with their potential in mind, I'll bet you'd give them many more opportunities.

With that in mind, I propose that the first key trait of a leader who wants to empower others is optimism. You must look favorably at your team, and have faith in their capacity for greatness. Assume potential even beyond your natural tendencies, and then see it as your job as a leader to help your team succeed. You can't assume failure and hope to be surprised.

I'm proposing a complete reframing of how you look at the people around you. You have to decide to commit to this renewed mindset today, and again tomorrow, and the day after that. You have to wipe the past clean and start again. This fresh start is what provides a foundation for trust that can build over time.

With this new assumption, we're going to do things a little differently this time to greatly improve the chances of others succeeding. Next I'll cover what true empowerment looks like.

SUMMARY

- A skeptical mindset, such as, "I don't think they can be as good as me," or, "People are problems," must be corrected.

- Assumptions are what you believe to be true without proof, which can drastically affect your response to people.

- It is worth questioning assumptions by looking at the facts, which is hard when it comes to assumptions about people.

- Assuming that others will always fail often comes from bad experiences that form the belief that all people will fail in the future.

- The result of a skeptical mindset is that you will not hand off important work or empower your team.

- If your default assumption is failure, your default response will be control.

- You must regain optimism in people and assume they will be successful; you can't assume failure and hope to be surprised.

- This fresh start is a foundation for trust that can build over time.

· See it as your job as a leader to set people up for success by empowering them in a way that significantly reduces the risk of failure.

Ask yourself: Do I assume that others will fail, even in subtle ways? How has it been a challenge for me to assume that people will be successful, and how has my past influenced any skeptical mindset?

- THREE -

STEPS TO EMPOWER

My education in empowerment began simply: with my kids at mealtime. I had a simple problem: I wanted them to wash their hands before eating. Easy, right?

Like most parents, I would naturally do one of two things to get their hands washed. The first way was drill-sergeant mode. (Now that I'm writing this, I can see that I'm sounding eerily similar to Coach. Not cool.)

I would see that the food was ready and call out to the playroom to tell my kids to wash their hands. It would start sweetly enough, usually with something like, "Time to wash hands, little buddies," in a loving tone. Then I might say, "Come wash your hands, dudes," still very nicely. Then I'd use a more neutral tone and a little more volume: "Wash your hands." And after that, I would typically break down and yell, "Get to the sink *now* before I . . ." Alright, you get the idea. (If you have kids, you know exactly what I'm talking about, so don't shake your head and go all judgmental parent on me now.)

If I wasn't giving a command, I would get my hands a little dirtier (or cleaner, if you will). I would take my kids' hands and put them under the water, add the soap, rub it off, and then dry them. That may be okay for a two-year-old, but for a four- and six-year-old, it was probably a little much.

However, one day I thought about the mealtime struggle and realized my sons could do a lot more if they were properly empowered. Looking at the situation, they could all reach the sink if there was a stepping stool close by. They would be able to put soap on their hands and rub them together under the water. They also had the mental capacity needed for this role.

I tried to help them understand the reason we washed our hands before we ate: so we didn't get sick (since being sick meant an early bedtime and less playing). And they also needed to know when the meal was almost ready so they could have enough notice to prepare.

It sounds basic, but I still needed to give them the responsibility of washing their hands before each meal. I had to stop telling them to go to the sink. I needed to give them the information they needed to own the role themselves. Then it would be on them to make decisions to achieve this goal.

After I had taken the time to give them responsibility, I saw some big changes. The kids would magically rush to wash their hands when we gave the word that supper was almost ready. The nearly inevitable pre-supper fight was over, which was nice. I was freed up from a very frustrating job of micromanaging.

I think the part I underestimated the most was the pride my kids took in owning their role. Much to my surprise, they did a great job without me. They beamed when I noticed them stepping up to the sink and told them I was impressed. My oldest especially grew in confidence as he started to take ownership of helping his younger brothers. Seeing the three kids line up at the sink without me was one of the greatest moments of my life. (Maybe I need to get out more.)

ELEMENTS OF EMPOWERMENT

Let me acknowledge that giving away power can be scary. It seems like so much can go wrong, far worse than dirty hands, but you should try to put this delegation of power in perspective. You're worried about letting people update a report or talk to a client, yet you drive next to rookie drivers on the road every day, where a single decision can mean the difference between life and death. So there must be a way to hand off power with confidence.

There are careless and wise ways to give away power. The careless way is to do it hastily and with little consideration. Imagine allowing someone to drive your car without a license. If something goes wrong with this ill-prepared driver, you might assume that all new drivers are failures, when in fact you created the problem by letting the person drive without following the proper steps.

To substantially increase the chances of seeing a successful result when you give this power away, three building blocks of empowerment must be present. I will refer back to these terms often in the rest of the book. The three crucial elements for empowerment are *Ability*, *Context*, and *Authority*.

Ability: what someone is good at.

Ability is a skill, strength, or proficiency. Using the driver's license comparison, Ability is having the mental capacity to comprehend the rules of the road. A driver must be able to react quickly to handle whatever may happen. Ability is also the obvious things like being able to turn the steering wheel or reach the pedals. In the case of my kids washing their hands, Ability is being able to reach the tap.

Context: what someone understands.

Context is information about a situation. It's knowledge and understanding. This would include knowing how to drive a car, knowing the rules of the road, and knowing why they're necessary. Context is also understanding what situations could arise. If I travel to a different area of the world, my Context will shift. In England, I would need to gain an understanding of how to drive on the opposite side of the road. My kids needed Context to know the reasons why handwashing matters and to get enough notice before a meal.

Authority: what someone owns.

Authority is the power part of empowerment. It is what people own or the responsibilities they have. Decisions can be made within that realm of ownership. Authority is represented by the driver's license that gives you the right to drive and make decisions for yourself in your vehicle. Notice, however, that the license comes only after the driving test, which makes sure that Ability and Context are established. I gave my kids Authority by giving them the responsibility for handwashing from then on.

All three elements must be present for empowerment to exist. It can be seen as a simple equation:

$$Empowerment = Ability + Context + Authority$$

If Ability is missing, you could have someone with full understanding and clear ownership who keeps doing a bad job. You will be frustrated, and the person will be annoyed by doing something he or she doesn't excel at.

If Context is missing, the person could be extremely skilled and have ownership, but then make bad judgment calls. If that happens, you will be frustrated that the person keeps making bad decisions and will think he or she just doesn't get it. And then you will likely revoke the Authority. Context is probably the most commonly absent element. Often times people blend Ability and Context together, even though Context is the real issue.

Finally, when Authority is missing, someone can have all the skills and knowledge but not be able to make autonomous decisions. This can be extremely frustrating for skilled, knowledgeable people; they believe they can excel on their own, but the leader doesn't let them.

Think about which of the three elements is lacking most with your team. I'll cover how to establish each element in detail in the next three chapters, but at this point it's helpful to have an initial idea of where your team stands.

NO SHORTCUTS

Now that we have a basic understanding of the three elements of empowerment, we can address how to empower someone.

Some people dislike that wording of empowering someone (maybe you're one of them). They say you can't empower others because a person must do it for him- or herself. While I agree, it's really just semantics. If you are the leader and you don't allow your team to make any decisions or have information, how are they going to be empowered? Only one way— they quit.

What I'm talking about is giving the people around you the option to choose to be empowered. They have the choice based on the options you make available. Can we call that empowering your team?

We're about to get into some intense material, so I want to warn you in advance about the time and effort involved in this empowerment process. The story of my kids washing their hands doesn't do it justice.

The initial stages of empowerment require enough time and effort to prepare you for sustainable, long-term, increased impact. You'll likely see a temporary reduction in productivity during this phase, before exponential increases follow. You can't take shortcuts or skimp. The degree to which you realize the benefits of empowerment depends on how much you choose to empower versus control. You must fully commit.

THE BIG ANNOUNCEMENT

Let's start with communication. You have to let the people around you know that you have seen the light and are now pursuing empowerment. This culture change will have a tremendous impact on your team, so you have to bring them in from the start. The content you'll share will essentially be a summarized version of this book. Here are the main points you'll have to cover and personalize.

The Problem

Begin by explaining the problems of your current approach. What are the limitations and barriers? You need to be clear about what drove you to make this change. Let people know your thought process. Maybe you are working long hours and can't get ahead. As a result, you don't have time to advance the business, and everyone is suffering. Or maybe you have realized that you're not putting people in positions where they can do their best work. You can even ask your team what problems they see, which brings them into the decision. That can be a very humbling yet powerful exercise.

The Solution

After the problem is clear, outline what empowerment means and will look like. What is empowerment and how will it work? The answers to this will become clearer as you read on. You'll inform your team that instead of telling people what to do, you'll now be providing Context and Authority. That means people on the team must go from a culture of robotically executing steps to thinking independently and taking ownership of their roles. This should help your team understand what will change for them specifically.

The Results

Finally, describe the results you plan on seeing because of this change. Paint a picture of what the future will look like once you take this approach. What are the benefits to you, the team, and the organization? Tell people that empowerment will put them in the driver's seat of their careers and help them reach their top potential. Describe the value of having a vibrant culture in which people are empowered and where they can achieve great things together. Explain that as a result of empowerment the team will be set up for success and the organization will be able to grow. This will bring opportunity to people who are ambitious and want to excel.

When you make this announcement, you'll likely see a mix of reactions. This change will raise the expectations for people to properly steward their Authority. Many people will think, "It's about time," and be thrilled about it. However, others may be concerned.

To those who just put in their time at work and don't want to think about their jobs, taking ownership won't be as appealing. (We'll cover more about this in the next chapter.) You hope they'll see the benefits and be eager to change; but if they don't, they need to know that the culture change is going to happen regardless. Empowerment isn't only for leaders; it's for everyone.

THREE STEPS

After you communicate the culture change, you have to carve out who owns what. You must have a vision for how Authority will be dispersed before you can empower your team.

This could seem like a daunting task, but I suggest starting simply. If you ask your team to describe what they think they are responsible for, this reduces your workload and brings them into the process. You might tweak and update their job descriptions but it's a starting point.

At this early phase of the transition, we mainly need a high-level summary with little detail. For example, you only need to know that Sam handles invoicing and payroll at this stage—nothing more.

When I first did this, I noticed just how loose things were. Even in the broadest terms, many people had trouble describing their roles, which again justifies why this process is so important.

The transition process might reveal the need to hire new staff. You could see that the team is overburdened. Or you might notice that certain jobs lack staffing but that your existing team is not qualified to do the work.

After clarifying the roles, you can walk through establishing the three elements of empowerment for each role. You need to ensure Ability, Context, and Authority are all in place. The steps look like this:

1. Ensure Ability: Make sure the person has the right skills.
2. Share Context: Provide information for complete understanding.
3. Delegate Authority: Hand over a clear area of ownership.

In other words, you need to engage people's strengths, share what they need to know, and hand over ownership.

This may sound simple, but it's amazing how often you can forget a step. You must be intentional to cover each step because at first it might not come naturally to you.

Leaders are usually thorough when hiring people and assigning their roles. But it's easy to be lazy with the steps for minor things, such as role changes or short-term projects, for example. Each step matters for all situations in which you are empowering someone.

Let's now dive into the first step: ensuring Ability.

SUMMARY

- Giving away power can be scary but there are careless and wise ways to do it.
- The three crucial elements for successful empowerment are Ability, Context, and Authority.
  - Ability: what someone is good at
  - Context: what someone understands
  - Authority: what someone owns
- If Ability is lacking, then the result will be poor quality work and you'll want to step in.
- Missing Context results in poor decisions and bad judgement calls, so you end up making all the decisions instead.
- When Authority isn't given to people, they aren't allowed to succeed.
- Empowerment initially requires a lot of time and effort before sustainable, long-term results occur.
- You must communicate this new culture change to your team, sharing the current problems, explaining why empowerment is the solution, and describing the benefits that will result.

- Every person on your team must embrace this culture of empowerment.

- After getting a rough idea of what each person on your team is responsible for, follow three steps to empower.

  - Ensure Ability: Make sure the person has the right skills.

  - Share Context: Provide information for complete understanding.

  - Delegate Authority: Hand over a clear area of ownership.

- To empower people, you must engage their strengths, share what they need to know, and hand over ownership.

Ask yourself: Which of the empowerment elements are lacking in my team? How will I introduce empowerment culture to my team?

- FOUR -

ENSURE ABILITY

The first step in empowering people is to make sure they have the necessary skills. Are they good at what they're about to own? To explain that, let me tell you a story in which the answer was a firm no.

A long time ago, I was in Costa Rica with my friend Brad. Cars with automatic transmissions were hard to come by, and unfortunately my skill at driving a stick-shift left much to be desired. Without the necessary skills, my driving was quite the spectacle for Brad, who literally had a front-row seat.

The whole ordeal came to a climax as we arrived at the resort where we were staying. I had to first stop at a security booth that had a relatively large speed bump right beside it. I nervously spoke to the attendant, knowing that I was about to need the magic clutch-and-gas combination that would get me started from a dead stop with my front tires pressed up against what might as well have been a brick wall.

The attendant cleared me to proceed. Then the inevitable happened. I tried to just go right at it with little thought, in the hopes that I might get lucky, but the result was a jolting of the car with the mountainous speed bump still before me. I started sweating, Brad put his head down, and worst of all, the security guard was still right next to me, staring disapprovingly.

On attempt number two, I took a little more time to visualize the plan before going for it, but got the same result. I expected the guard to look away and pretend not to notice what was happening. He could have picked up the newspaper next to him to fake read with one eye and glare at me with the other. But alas, he continued to stare straight at me.

To make a long, painful story short, I had one more failed attempt, at which point I wanted to die. Brad never let me drive after that, and he certainly hasn't let me live it down.

SKILLS DECONSTRUCTED

This first step toward empowering people is the simplest, but simple doesn't mean insignificant. It may seem obvious, especially if you have competent, talented people around you. But you could be in for a lot of frustration if you don't give considerable attention to Ability. Your team could end up looking like my attempts to drive in Costa Rica. And you could be sitting in the security booth shaking your head.

For example, you could put someone in a client-relations position who is friendly but who isn't thorough. When she's on the phone with clients, they love her, but she often forgets to call someone or misses key check-ins. Next thing you know, you're asking her every day who she called and who she is planning to call. Eventually you assume more control, telling her who to call and providing checklists of what to cover.

These gaps in Ability only show up when you assess what skills are needed to fulfill a role. Saying someone is good at client relations isn't detailed enough. That's too intangible. When you think broadly like this, you typically focus on what you deem to be the most important skill, such as being friendly, but you overlook all the other key strengths needed to do the job well. Breaking down the necessary skills will better allow you to put people in positions that they are good at, and also figure out what might be lacking if something goes awry.

PRESERVE YOUR SANITY

Once you've listed the required skills, then you can decide what to do if a person is missing one or two of them. What happens when you have a salesperson who isn't good at written communication? What if his emails are terrible?

One option is to help him improve. I know it's debatable how much a person can improve at certain skills. You'll have to assess the investment you're willing to make, which depends on the person, the specific skill, and the gap that exists. You could encourage the person to take writing classes, but you may also not be interested in going that far if the emails are *that* bad.

If the emails aren't horrible, maybe some practice could help. So instead of official training, informal help could be offered. Someone who is good at writing could proofread work done by the salesperson and give feedback. He could remain in his role as head of sales but just have a temporary limitation that will go away when the writing improves.

Or maybe the salesperson could spend some time reviewing emails by other people who are great at writing. Maybe he could even take the first stab at writing emails for other people, to have more opportunity to practice. These are just a few ideas of how you could help someone in this area. The bottom line is that you are choosing to help the person. You are giving time and effort to help him get better at a skill.

In some cases, the position just isn't right for a person. In these cases, give the role to someone else (if you value your sanity). If Ability isn't there, empowerment will not work, period. Ability is the foundation for empowering someone. Putting people in roles where they lack the necessary skills will lead to poor-quality work. That could then make you feel like you have to micromanage the situation, which you don't want. You either help people improve or help them transition somewhere else.

I primarily hire based on shared values, so I will help people switch roles if they are a solid cultural fit with the company. It's too hard to find people who care about the same things I do, so I don't want to let them go when I find them.

I also try to empower people in areas that are more aligned with their skill sets. For the salesperson who is bad at writing, I might place him in a position that requires less written and more verbal communication, such as a phone-based customer support position. Obviously, the person must be interested in the change, but it's a win-win if the new role is aligned with his skills.

STIR THE MEAT

Even if Ability is there, that doesn't mean someone is empowered. In fact, control is based on taking someone's Ability and leveraging it to accomplish a specific task or purpose (albeit usually a reduced percentage of someone's Ability). For example, you could put a kid who doesn't know the rules of the road behind the wheel and just tell him or her what to do the whole time: stop here, move to the right lane now, slow down, and so on.

People may also choose to not be empowered even if they have all the necessary skills. I've seen talented people at work who don't want to gain real understanding or be in decision-making roles. And to be honest, I can relate to those people in some situations in my own life.

For example, I've never been interested in cooking. In theory I might have the skills, but I'll probably never know because I'm not that interested in applying myself in this area. Fortunately, my wife is great at cooking and loves making new things.

The other day, she asked me to stir some meat on the stove while she left the kitchen for a minute. Those were her instructions: stir the meat. (Take note of the wording, as it will become very important.) So, what do you think I did? I stirred the meat. However, there was one small issue: the meat started to burn.

Meanwhile, my brain was on another planet, likely thinking about empowerment or maybe coming up with amazing new ideas that could save the world. I tend to be selective about reserving my brainpower for only certain things, and cooking is not on that list.

As you may recall, I wasn't asked to turn the stove off when the meat started to burn, or to cook the meat to the perfect juiciness. I was specifically asked to stir the meat. (I'm sure that many people are rolling their eyes right now, pretending they don't get what I'm saying.) When my wife returned, do you think she thanked me for stirring the meat exactly as she requested? We all know the answer to that question.

The point is, I believe I have the Ability to contribute in the kitchen, but I'm not willing to be empowered. Oddly enough, I prefer to be controlled in the kitchen, and to be told exactly what to do without having to think about how to do it myself. I don't want to know how everything is made or to make decisions.

I'm the same way with directions. When my wife is in the car, I set my brain on autopilot and execute the turns she tells me to make. We'll be driving to a friend's house for the third time, and I'll have no idea how to get there. This causes my wife to have a similar reaction as when I was stirring the meat.

(Can I save face a little and say that try to be very helpful during mealtime despite not wanting to be empowered? I am a force to be reckoned with when it comes to brainless things like doing the dishes, cleaning up messes, and so on. Plus, you can't forget who empowered the kids to wash their hands. That's all helpful stuff, right?)

As I mentioned earlier, there may be some people on your team who aren't willing to be empowered. They may prefer to put in their nine-to-five each day and be given clear instructions. You have to decide whether there is a place for these types of people in your organization, but personally I want team members who want to be empowered. I want people who are eager to understand what they are doing and to have the power to make decisions. This kind of team does the best work and allows real growth for the organization, so I don't compromise here.

Once we have confirmed Ability and know that a person is interested in being empowered, then we can move on to step two: sharing Context.

SUMMARY

- The first step toward empowering people is to make sure they have the necessary skills.

- You must consider if each person on your team is good at all aspects of what they own.

- The required skills for a role should be broken down to make sure team members have all the skills they need to perform well. For example, avoid saying someone is good at client relations in general, and look for friendliness, organization, reliability, etc.

- If a person lacks the necessary skills, you must assess the gap that exists and how much you are willing to invest in helping the person learn.

- Ability must be present for empowerment to work, so unless you are willing to help, don't leave people in positions where they won't thrive.

- You can help grow Ability by training, encouraging practice, and having a designated period of time during which aspects of work will be reviewed for feedback.

- You should try to align roles with strengths, empowering in the areas of greatest Ability.

· Ability alone does not mean empowerment, as control is based on leveraging someone's skills for piecemeal tasks.

· People must be willing to use their Ability to be empowered.

Ask yourself: Do people on your team currently have roles that align with their skills? How can I best help people grow in Ability?

- FIVE -

SHARE CONTEXT

I started my company in my early twenties. It was 2004, and I was on vacation with my family in Florida. (When I say family, I don't mean wife and kids—I mean my parents, because at that time I was the kid.) While we were there, I met up with a friend for lunch—a guy named Jason who worked in disaster recovery for the Florida state government.

He told me about the devastation caused by a hurricane that had struck the Florida coast and the massive amount of paperwork the state would have to process, including an unprecedented number of requests to get financial help, to help communities rebuild. The recovery team was worn out, working seven days a week, twelve hours a day.

Jason seemed to be thinking out loud when he asked if I could help with some sort of software solution. I thought the idea sounded interesting, so he offered to introduce me to Del, the person in charge of the recovery effort.

There I was at twenty-three, walking into Del's office with no product to show and long hair and an eyebrow ring that told the world I wasn't ready to be a businessman yet, to ask for his trust on a long-shot idea. To make a long story less long, he miraculously said yes, which changed the trajectory of my life in a hurry. Overnight the company MB3 was born.

I spent a week driving with Jason to the hardest-hit areas of the state, surveying the damage firsthand. I saw entire communities nearly wiped out, met with city and county officials, and listened as Jason explained how the state was going to help with the recovery efforts. I not only learned about the problem but also became passionate about finding a way to help get people's lives back together.

I was set up with a cubicle right in the middle of the office. I overheard discussions and was part of impromptu meetings that further helped me learn the state's processes. I also capitalized on any spare moment I could get with Del, which usually meant joining him on smoke breaks. I remember holding myself back from choking, trying to look cool and be one of the guys. I was willing to take a hit for the team if it helped me learn something that would help me be successful.

Over a six-month period, I worked in my little cubicle, building the product just fast enough to stay ahead of where the state was in the process. I joined the rest of the team working inhumane hours, and became known as the kid in socks who did magical stuff on my computer that saved the day. I was also in Florida as three more hurricanes made landfall that year. I got to experience it all.

One time, a city manager called the state to complain about not having money that was promised, which I think was around $10 million dollars. I asked to take the call. I heard her concerns, worked to make sure the software gave her clearer status reports, and tried to expedite the process even more. She became a voice that motivated me to build something great. I wanted her life to be better.

After this experience slowed down, I got a chance to relax for about two months. Then Hurricane Katrina happened, which devastated New Orleans and the surrounding areas. I wasn't ready for the software to transfer beyond Florida, but that didn't stop it from happening. I hit the road again and spent the next six months driving between Louisiana, Mississippi, and Alabama, which was even more exhausting than Florida with the grueling late-night driving.

Once again, experiencing what clients went through was an incredible opportunity. But in this case, I really saw a direct link between the software and the damage. When I first arrived in New Orleans, I remember the eerie feeling of driving downtown in the pitch black of a city without power. I could just barely see the Superdome that I had seen so many times on the news, and I knew the repairs to the building would be managed using the product I was working on. I stayed in the only hotel room I could find in operation.

I drove through communities where every single house had been destroyed. Block after block, people's homes showed waterline imprints around the second story. They were moldy and uninhabitable inside, abandoned, and waiting to be demolished. I must have seen thousands of cars abandoned on the sides of roads, destroyed by floodwater and debris.

I could go on, but here's my question and the point of this story: How could I possibly bottle up all those experiences and share them with my team? How could other people gain the Context I had?

The honest answer is that for years I made no effort to share what I knew and experienced. I kept hiring people who were further and further removed from those days, and I expected them to do great work. I had talented, skilled people who were working on a product they didn't fully understand. They had a limited vision of the disaster's impact on the ground, and they didn't fully understand that tens of billions of dollars were managed in the system that they were working on.

Because I didn't share these experiences, how could I possibly expect my team to be empowered to do great work? How could they make good decisions? My decisions, of course, would almost always be better. And as I saw the pattern of my decisions being the best, I strengthened the assumption that I *was* the best.

Let's explore what it looks like to share the Context your team needs to succeed.

FROM JAZZ TO BLUES

The second step in empowering someone is to share Context. This is making sure people know and understand what they need to in order to take on Authority, the third and final step that will be covered in the next chapter.

If you find the word "Context" confusing, here's an analogy that might help. Think of pulling a sentence out of a book. The more you read before and after that sentence, the more it makes sense. For example, let's say you shared the following sentence of this book with someone who hasn't read it: "I even saw him kiss his flexed bicep a couple of times." Not only would the person decide to never read this book, but he or she would also, and, more relevantly to this comparison, be very confused. The more sentences that are revealed, the more that particular sentence would make sense. Providing Context means sharing as much of the book as possible to help people completely understand the part they are reading.

In controlling environments there is usually little valuable Context provided; it's mainly step-by-step instructions. If you needed directions, I could say, "Turn left, then take the second right, and then watch for the two-story building on the right."

Empowerment does the opposite—few detailed instructions but all the surrounding information. It's a transfer of knowledge and experience. Instead of dictating each turn for you, I could give you a map, show you the destination, mark areas to avoid, and provide tips about best routes. This allows people to make their own decisions. Providing your team with Context is the foundation that gives you the confidence to hand over ownership.

Sharing Context is like providing a driver's handbook to a new driver before he or she gets behind the wheel. Or taking a driver's education program that gives people real experience on the road. I shared context with my kids when I explained all the reasons why we should wash our hands before we eat, and by showing them the best techniques to kill the maximum number of germs. The friendly, helpful customer-service person would probably need to understand the products and know about the clients, at the very least, to be successful.

While Ability is about being skilled to do something *in general,* Context allows you to apply these skills to *a specific situation or setting.* This is similar to a great jazz guitarist switching to a blues band. The person has the guitar skills, but the way to apply the skills changes when playing a different music genre. Context is an understanding of the new setting in order to fully use Ability.

It is important to note that it's not just having the information that matters—it's fully understanding it. Context enables people to know *why,* not just *what.* When Context is present, your team should never be able to say either of these two things:

a) I don't understand, but I have to do it anyway.

b) I didn't know about that, and it affects me.

Just think of the feeling that people must have if they constantly don't understand what they're doing. It can make people feel out of control, frustrated, and deflated. I'd probably just shut my brain off. When this happens, the job isn't about doing great work; it's about putting in time and punching a clock. But if people are always aware of what's going on and fully understand, you'll see all the benefits of empowerment.

Sharing Context usually takes the most time of the three empowerment steps. It's obviously a lot faster to give someone the exact steps of what to do than to take the time to help someone understand. But I see a direct correlation between Context and great decisions and ideas.

WHERE IS THE LINE?

Some people wonder how far to take this whole Context-sharing thing. How much Context is enough? Where is the line? After all, there is a lot of information people could learn, and we have to be practical since there isn't an infinite amount of time to work with.

Since the right amount of Context is subjective, here are some questions that will help you make a decision:

- How often is variation possible? Is it likely that unforeseen circumstances will come up? If so, Context will allow a person to navigate beyond predictable steps.

- How complex or creative is the role? Is it a complicated role or one that needs creativity to come up with solutions? If so, Context brings much needed understanding.

- Do you want people's ideas? Or are you looking for something to be done the same way it is currently being done? If you want ideas, more Context will give people more information to draw from.

- Is this a long-term role? A one-time task requires less Context and therefore less investment from the leader. But if this is a long-term role, Context is crucial.

People only know what's in their world or what you allow to be in their world. They can't know the full picture of sales, finance, operations, and so on unless you help them learn. Let's say you walk into a product design meeting right after a meeting with the sales team. You propose a great update to the product in the exact area customers care the most about. Is that a genius idea that only you could come up with? Maybe, but that's only by your own design. The main reason you came up with the idea was your access to Context. All the other people in the meetings only knew about their own worlds whereas you had the unique advantage of a bird's-eye view.

When someone suggests an idea that seems ridiculous, it's often because the person didn't have the Context to know it wouldn't work. If someone makes a bad decision, it's frequently because he or she lacked the information they needed to make a good one.

Let me be clear. Problems with your team are often caused by leaders who fail to equip people properly. Team members can only draw from the knowledge and understanding they have in their heads. Thoughts and ideas don't just come out of thin air. It's on you to set them up for success with more Context and to foster an environment where people are encouraged to put themselves out there. (I'll cover that topic later in the "Reinforce Empowerment" chapter.)

How big is the world you are creating for the people around you? The more you open up their worlds, the more they can think and contribute. Are they positioned to come up with great ideas and not just maintain something?

ALL THE SMELLS

So back to my story and what I did when I finally became aware of the Context gap. I started by trying to get every person in the company to visit a client and see some of the things I saw firsthand. It wasn't easy since our clients were in different cities, but I remember the impact it made. People who had worked for the company for years suddenly felt as if they understood the reason for our work.

It was fascinating to see the things that people picked up about client offices that they never knew: the pictures and maps on the walls, the type of computers, and even what the building smelled like. They also learned a lot about the people: their appearance, how social they were, and the size of the team. These are all things that may seem unimportant for a software developer, but now the team knew who they were making the software for. And this can make a difference when designing or troubleshooting.

I remember a situation in which one team member came back from a client visit concerned that we needed to respond to support tickets faster. He was with someone when part of the product wasn't working properly, so he helped submit a support ticket. The client was at a standstill while waiting for the ticket to be resolved, and the guy on my team felt that pain. He could relate and had empathy. He was now an advocate for the client's happiness. We discussed his experiences as a team so everyone could hear his stories and see his photos.

To gain client access, I would often allow anyone interested to listen in on my calls. This gave people exposure to a lot of valuable Context. After the calls, we would discuss thoughts and questions, which was also a great learning experience.

COMPANY 101

In addition to gaining client experience, I also got into more traditional training methods, like a visual company 101 that started with the basic company information.

For example, the company had a one-sentence mission statement, but I found that people needed layers of Context before they could understand it, let alone pursue it. You'd first have to know that the industry even exists. Then you could get into the details about it. Beyond that, there's business-specific language, the purpose of the product, some history, the competition, and more. It's a lot.

To address this, I thought about ways to help people understand. I included pictures of the New Orleans Superdome before and after the rebuild and described the exact details of where MB3's product fit in the process, allowing my team to grasp what the company was about.

The company's vision, and the purpose of the product, became clear. This information became part of the initial orientation of any new employee in the company. I personally presented the information so that I could share my experiences and answer questions. These resources took time to create and present, but I believe the empowerment of my team depended on that investment.

When the overall picture of the company is understood, an intentional training path can be followed to fill in the details. When going deeper into some material, I personally enjoy interactive group discussion. Many people learn through conversation and talking things through. I like to get a few people in a room and ask relatively vague questions first to get the discussion started. For example, I might ask how communities receive money for rebuilding. I then serve as a discussion moderator, encouraging them to challenge peers and express opinions. Once the debate is over, often when the group reaches a consensus, I'll weigh in by providing feedback and guidance.

For months I hosted weekly discussions to help people grow in their understanding of the business. To start each session, I would ask a randomly selected person to step up to the whiteboard and walk through what they'd learned so far. This was a way for them to practice presenting the material while the rest of the group tried to spot issues. The whole team became quite fluent in subject matter that was previously only understood by two or three people in the company, which paid huge dividends.

CULTURE GUIDES

I'm now going to touch on a subject that really could have an entire book written about it: culture. Every person on your team needs to have the Context for how you expect people to act.

The word "culture" gets thrown around in a lot of ways—people have very different ideas about what it actually means. In many cases, culture is seen as office perks, like retro arcade games and catered lunches.

Stated simply, culture is how a group of people thinks and acts. A fancy coffee machine can hint at the culture or even influence the culture, but it isn't culture in and of itself. I believe that meaningful culture is less tangible, like how people work together and see each other. Most companies do a very poor job of laying out what behaviors they're looking for.

So, the question is, how do we influence culture in the right way? What Context should you share related to culture?

Some organizations choose to implement excessive rules and policies, overly restricting the actions people can take. For example, a company might require five approvals to send a sales email or to make a product update. This bureaucracy is especially common in larger organizations that grow beyond the point of being able to supervise every person's actions, or needing to hire beyond a tightly-knit founding team. But this approach often limits creativity, shuts down ideas, and slows progress.

Other organizations take the opposite approach, leaving actions to chance. Some people are rude, unreliable, or extremely unproductive, and such behavior is tolerated with no apparent repercussions. Even though this anything-goes culture could sound appealing on the surface, most people who value doing a good job won't last in that environment.

Some workplaces even mix the two approaches. In certain areas there are rules for everything, but in other areas there is chaos. Government offices often have a lot of red tape and inflexible rules, while management styles are all over the map and colleagues are unreliable.

Empowerment requires clarity of Context. It can be achieved many ways, but let me tell you my preference. I believe core values should be the single greatest influence on culture, not as an exhaustive list of rules, but more as the template from which to make sound decisions. Culture is a by-product, in a sense, of values. For example, if one of your values is caring for people, then actions should demonstrate that people matter.

Every day you and your team will learn more about how to apply your values. When you learn something new, write it down; not as a rule, but as Context to help others in the future. In my case, I worked with my team to produce a culture guide summarizing the culture we desired, which we even made available for job applicants. We captured the resources that I had shared over the years, adding to our collective knowledge as a team.

AN ONGOING CONVERSATION

Before wrapping up the subject of sharing Context, I want to briefly cover a concern many have over this Context-driven approach. You may notice that even after sharing a lot of information, the lack of instructions and rules leaves a lot open to interpretation when it comes to spelling out how to act and what to do. For example, what does it look like to care about the well-being of others or to be reliable? Or what exactly should a support person do with an angry customer on the phone? Those topics alone could be addressed with pages of policies, and it's tempting to implement steps and rules to add clarity. But a healthy empowerment culture cannot be sustained without honest, ongoing feedback.

Each person, from the CEO to the development team to reception, must be completely open to receive feedback and have a desire to improve. There should be an ongoing conversation within the team for the pursuit of excellence. Everyone has a stake in making sure the culture is an accurate reflection of your core values, and producing incredible work.

I'll stop here for now and will cover more about living out of culture and providing feedback in the upcoming "Lead" section.

Again, sharing Context might seem like a massive undertaking, but you're positioning people for success. Context is the basis for sound decisions, which allows you to hand over ownership. It's short-term pain for long-term gain.

What do you need to share with each person on your team for them to be successful? Be creative when coming up with ways to transfer knowledge. Sharing Context is your challenge to solve, but you must solve it if you want to give away Authority, which I'll cover next.

SUMMARY

- The second step in empowering someone is to share Context.

- Sound decisions come from Context which prepares someone to take on Authority.

- Control uses step-by-step instructions whereas empowerment provides background information and experiences.

- Ability is about being skilled to do something in general; Context allows you to apply skills to a specific situation or setting.

- Context must be known and understood to be valuable (why, not just what).

- When Context is present, your team should never be able to say:

    - I don't understand but I have to do it anyway.

    - I didn't know about that, and it affects me.

- Sharing Context is typically the most time-consuming step in empowerment since it's easier to share exact steps than to help someone understand enough to come up with a plan.

- To figure out how much Context to share, ask if variation is likely, if the work is complex/creative, if you are wanting ideas, and if this a longer-term role.

- You must figure out creative ways of sharing Context so your team is positioned to thrive, from resources to interactive training and experiences.

- Culture is an important piece of Context that must be outlined, including expectations for how people work together.

- A healthy Context-driven empowerment culture cannot be sustained without ongoing honest feedback.

Ask yourself: What Context do I need to share to see my team empowered? What is the best way I can share?

- SIX -

DELEGATE AUTHORITY

Now that a solid foundation of Ability and Context exists, Authority can be confidently handed over. Can you see how giving away power is less scary at this point? It might seem as if this last step will just naturally fall into place now that the foundation of empowerment has been established, but you have to see the process through.

Delegating Authority is when an official gives you a license to drive. When I gave my kids the responsibility to wash their hands, I transferred authority to them.

I think there is an epidemic of unclear ownership in organizations. Often it comes down to vague expectations, even though a leader might incorrectly think the roles within their team are obvious.

Let's say I ask you to help with a project. Do you know if I've officially transferred the project to you? Do you know your exact part and what is expected of you?

Consider the people on your team and what you think they own. Do you think they could clearly articulate their areas of responsibility? Most people need extreme clarity to feel a sense of ownership and to really contribute within their areas.

I believe delegation of Authority requires defining two main things:

- What is owned—what a person is being given power over
- What is expected—what the results should be, including the timeline

It's similar to purchasing a piece of land, which I recently did. I signed a contract that included a detailed map showing exact coordinates. I could walk the property and see the corner posts in the ground. I knew exactly what I was going to own.

Also, part of the contract included the expectation that I would build a house within a specific timeframe. I could use any builder I wanted, but the house had to have a minimum square footage. That is what was expected of me, which came with the ownership I was taking on. I could design any house of my choosing that met the specifications in the contract.

That is the kind of clarity that exists for purchasing land, and I believe transferring Authority in organizations should be comparable.

WHAT IS OWNED

Let's go into more detail, starting with what is owned. I'll use an office manager as an example here. The problem is that the title of office manager provides very little information about ownership. Does the office manager manage people? Does that person manage the office facilities? Instead I could be more specific by listing things such as stocking office supplies, booking travel, and approving leave requests. That's a start in carving out the exact aspects of what's being owned.

What is owned also includes the available resources. For example, the office manager might be given monthly budgets for office supplies and lunches, while travel bookings can be booked when flight prices are below a certain threshold. These are basically preapproved spending limits.

Resources could also be people who can be called on to help. Being an owner of a role doesn't mean one person has to execute everything within that area alone. That person does ultimately have responsibility, but parts can be delegated as it makes sense (using the same three empowering steps, no doubt).

These owned areas can be broadened as a person grows in Ability and Context as well. For example, a budget cap can be expanded as someone gains experience and trust is developed. We'll cover more about making these adjustments later in the book, but for now we're handing out Authority based on the current scenario.

WHAT IS EXPECTED

Establishing clear expectations is probably the more complicated part of carving out ownership. It's related to the desired results. It's what success, or the ideal outcome, looks like. What it's *not* is instructions on exactly how to do something. I sometimes refer to outcome-driven requests as communicating intent. What do you intend to happen?

I could ask the office manager to book a specific flight, but what I really want is the flight with the shortest travel time. I could ask for meals to be ordered from only a couple places, but what I really want is a healthy option. Providing a little Context will empower the person to use his or her skills to achieve the goal. If you pay attention to this, you'll very often hear people communicating specifics instead of their intent.

At the airport, you could ask if seat 15A is available. But the Context you didn't share was that your friend is in the seat beside that one, so you would like to sit together. That's the intent or desired outcome, to sit with your friend who is in 15B, and there are multiple ways to achieve that. Options can be severely limited by the way you ask.

As another example, let's say you are having a graphic prepared for some marketing material, and you don't like part of it. The natural reaction is to ask to change a title to a larger font or change the colors, but the intent is really to have a key phrase stand out more. You say, "Can you make the font bigger?" but what you should say is, "What do you think is the best way to make this phrase stand out?" Do you see the difference? Then the graphic designer can leverage his or her Ability to do an amazing job of accomplishing that intent.

Back to the office manager: The desired outcome for supplies is to always have an adequate amount available within a given budget. It really doesn't matter how that happens, although purchases are ideally made where a corporate account exists. For team lunches, success might be healthy food with a lot of variety for a reasonable price. There's no need to limit more than that. Let the person be creative and figure it out.

One caution here is that you will need to be flexible about exactly how the outcome is achieved. You can't criticize every step in the process, providing the desired result happens.

This is what my three-year-old needed when we were building a tower. We both wanted a tall tower in the end. But he wasn't flexible as to how we would achieve that goal. You may want four blocks at the base of the tower, but if your team wants six, and that makes for a sturdy foundation to build a great tower, you need to stay out of it.

In some roles, the definition of success is connected to metrics. For example, the desired result for sales could be a pipeline of a certain dollar amount, including a weekly report of the most promising ten accounts. This report is then available to you and the team to track at a bird's-eye view.

What is expected should also include a timeline for project- or task-based roles. Typically, the most important date is the due date. You should provide Context as to why the date matters and make it clear that the desired result must be done by that date. For example, if there is a new initiative to replace the lobby furniture, the due date could be based on an important client coming to visit the office, which is Context you would share as part of the transfer of ownership.

The timeline should also include status updates that you may want. The frequency of these updates depends on the level of trust you've developed with a certain person. If someone is relatively new, you could ask for more frequent updates, but once a person proves to be dependable, the updates should be less often (or even disappear completely). An update could be based on a certain date, such as the halfway mark of a project, or it could be based on a trigger event or milestone, such as a project that is tracking over budget.

Whatever frequency you set, the idea is for you to not ever have to check in. People should own their role and check in with you according to the established parameters. We'll talk about the importance of sticking to these dates a little later on in the book.

A COLLABORATIVE PROCESS

We have now talked about all the details with which to establish what is owned and what is expected. Let's talk now about how the delegation part works.

I believe clear ownership starts with what I call a *distinct moment*. This is a specific time when you discuss ownership and the details surrounding it. You can't walk by someone in the hallway and assign a project (or at the urinals, as I already so eloquently covered).

We have an ongoing joke around the office about whether two people had their distinct moment. I realize the phrase sounds a little weird, as if you need to schedule an intimate candlelit dinner, but the idea is to deliberately carve out a time and place to discuss the specifics of handing something off.

So far in this chapter I may have implied that it is up to you to outline every detail of ownership. However, whenever possible, I suggest encouraging the other person to participate in carving out the ownership as a collaborative process. When the person contributes, the role is much clearer to him or her and brings a lot more buy-in right from the start. For example, it's more powerful for the other person to set a due date than for you to dictate one. The person will be more likely to remember the date and own it.

Also, it's tedious to run through ownership checklists with the key people I frequently work with every time a small project comes along. As I gain trust in these people, we agree to shift the responsibility for establishing these criteria to the owner of the project. This shift allows me to be more vague when describing a project, where people come to me to fill any gaps they have. Eventually you want everyone fighting for clarity of what they own.

CHOCOLATE ON YOUR NOSE

This leads to my last point about delegating Authority. If you want an empowered team that cares about the organization as a whole, I strongly suggest sharing broader Authority so that people have influence outside the borders of their roles. Especially given all the Context you've shared, I'd expect you to want their feedback and ideas about any area.

Shared ownership over the whole organization allows everyone to contribute to its overall success. I ask for proactive ideas and delegate Authority to people to bring feedback about anything they see. This is all part of their ownership.

This type of culture takes time to develop. People might assume that speaking up could negatively affect their jobs. You have to be clear that you want honest feedback and then foster that freedom among your team.

Some leaders try to keep people quiet and don't entertain suggestions from anyone. This doesn't make sense to me. If you were eating dessert and got some chocolate on your nose, would you want someone to tell you? Or would you prefer to just keep walking around with a mess on your face? If you suppress the voices of your team, then you probably have chocolate on your face, and a lot of people notice. (But at least you keep your pride, right?)

What if someone notices an area of the business that isn't aligned with the vision? What if the values aren't being lived out in every area? Or what if someone sees an issue in another department? Wouldn't you want these things brought forward?

On a more positive note, what if a customer-service person has ideas for market expansion based on spending hours each day with living, breathing customers? Wouldn't you want to hear from that person? This broad Authority for ideas could be the next multi-million-dollar branch of the company.

The concept of *the best idea wins* became very popular with my team. People love being able to share ideas and to contribute to key decisions. We all try to leave our biases at the door and to reach the absolute best outcome, regardless of the seniority of the people in the room. This process also brings tremendous buy-in for the final decision.

That was a lot of material—are you still with me? We covered the three steps for your team to be empowered: ensure Ability, share Context, and delegate Authority.

With that, your team is fully empowered. So that's it, right? Time to take that sailing trip around the world like you've always wanted? Not quite; your team needs real leadership first.

SUMMARY

- Now that a solid foundation of Ability and Context exist, Authority can be confidently handed over.
- Delegation of Authority includes two key elements:
    - What is owned - What a person is being given to have power over (exact areas owned including available resources).
    - What is expected - What the results should be (includes desired outcome and timeline).
- Communicating intent involves specifying the desired end result, not the steps to get there.
- You must be flexible with the way in which the end result is achieved.
- Tying metrics to role expectations allows you to monitor results at a glance instead of getting into details.
- A timeline must be established in advance that allows you to avoid initiating status updates.
- There should be a "distinct moment" where it is very clear what ownership is being transferred.

- When discussing ownership, involve the person who is accepting responsibility for their input, buy-in, and understanding.

- Delegate broad Authority for feedback and ideas beyond the borders of exact roles.

- It should be the responsibility of every person to see the organization succeed.

Ask yourself: Are there areas where I haven't clearly delegated Authority for roles, projects, or even more broadly? How can I do a better job at transferring ownership?

PART TWO

LEAD

- SEVEN -

MANAGER VERSUS LEADER

I've been obsessed with a simple question for a while: What does a leader actually do? What should *I* do with my time? I don't mean some vague altruistic idea that a leader motivates, inspires, or does other intangible stuff you hear so much about. But when I get to work at 8:57 a.m., what do I do? Then at 9:04 a.m.? You get the idea.

If you randomly poll a few people off the street and ask them what a leader does, you'll likely get variations of these two answers: A leader solves all the problems, or a leader tells people what to do. So, leaders do stuff or tell people to do stuff (a.k.a. control).

Within a world of control, there's always a lot for the person in charge to do. People constantly need to be told what to do. Decisions need to be made. And urgent work needs to be done. But what about with an empowered team? What happens then?

ACCENT SUPERPOWERS

I was recently driving along the coast of South Africa with my friend Christo. I thought he was the perfect person to ask about how to lead an empowered team because he coaches successful leaders for a living. He actually used to be my coach, until we became friends; which means I now get his life-changing advice for free.

I jumped right into the conversation. "What does the word 'leader' mean to you? I mean, so many people have different opinions about exactly what a leader is, and I'm just wondering about your take."

"Yeah, I have thoughts," he said contemplatively. "The way I see it, a leader is someone who walks somewhere with people following behind."

You need to know that Christo is originally from South Africa, and he has an accent that makes him sound about ten times smarter than regular people like me. His accent is almost like having a superpower, especially in the world of coaching. He could say something ridiculous, such as, "A leader is a place that walks blue with three aliens," and it would sound transformational.

He delayed for a moment and then continued. "And a person whom people *want* to follow, not because they have to."

I was impressed with his answer, although it was a little hard to know just how impressive it was given the accent. Plus, the scenery was spectacular on the winding road that led to Cape Town, with mountains on one side of the road and the ocean on the other. Still, I wanted to go further into the topic. I asked, "But is the leader always in front?"

"Could be in front, or behind," he said with an even larger pause.

I wasn't going to let him get off easily with such a vague answer. He continued, "Depends on what's needed at the time."

His response had the illusion of substance, but it wasn't quite there for me.

He asked, "What's your definition?"

After working with Christo for a long time, I'm on to his tricks. He pulls this veteran coach move where he responds to a question with a question. I'll ask what to do about something and he'll respond with, "What do *you* think you should do about it?" Even when I think I've exhausted my thoughts and want him to tell me the answer, he'll keep creating more space by using his patented, and very annoying, line: "What's coming up for you now?"

Next thing I know, I've figured it out on my own, only to wonder why I needed his help in the first place. But then, an hour later, I'm convinced I need his help on something else and wholeheartedly believe I must talk to him. It's like a Jedi mind trick.

Despite knowing all this, I still fell for it. "I think a leader is someone who invests in other people and gets the best out of them." I liked my answer as I was saying it, but upon reflection I thought it was missing something. "There also has to be a common goal. You have to be heading somewhere together, which requires the best from everyone," I said.

"Yes, definitely," he said, indicating I should continue.

"But I guess helping people achieve their best is kind of self-serving, since as a leader you tend to care the most about reaching a goal. And if the team is excelling, that goal is achieved sooner. But I think the whole team wins by being in an environment where people give their best and grow in the process."

Christo stepped in. "People want to be empowered, I think," he said.

I didn't realize it at the time, but he had used *my* word to answer my question, and I was somehow impressed. See what I mean about next-level coaching?

He brought the conversation back to the real subject. "Leaders also need to create clarity around goals."

I thought for a second. "I personally don't think it matters what the goal is. I think people want to give their best and do something amazing together. And that's on the leader to set them up for that."

Christo picked up where I'd left off. "Yeah, a leader needs to create the right context. Or the setting. Or the . . ." His voice trailed off for a split second, as if he was trying to find the word.

"Environment!" I said, as if I was trying to win a guess-the-missing-word contest.

"A leader creates the right conditions and brings people along to do something great together," he said.

"Hold on," I said abruptly. "I have to write that down: A leader creates the right conditions." I wrote this on my phone knowing that I would definitely be stealing it. "That's key."

Christo went on. "Everyone needs a leader or coach to be successful." But then he corrected himself. "Perhaps not everyone. It depends on your definition of success. But to excel, people need someone looking out for their best interests, pushing them forward, caring about them, and helping them achieve their best."

Right then we pulled up to the place where he was dropping me off, and just like that the conversation was over.

CREATING THE RIGHT CONDITIONS

Let me explain what I mean when I use the word "leader." Most of the time, the term leader is considered to be a title or one's rank in an organization. However, in my opinion, being a CEO doesn't mean you're a leader. Being a CEO makes you a person with a big title who can choose whether or not to be a leader.

When I use the word "leader," usually I'm referring to a role, not a title. It's defined by what you do, not what position you hold. So, if true leaders don't tell people what to do and make big decisions, what do they do? What could be left?

After empowering a team, the role of a leader is to support others. It's a modest role, which is why it is rare to see people operating this way. You play a supporting role, and your team members are the heroes. You elevate others so they shine. Your leadership mindset is to exist for the benefit of others. That is a leader—not a title or position of being in charge.

Instead of making statements, you ask questions. You defend the Authority you've given people and look for opportunities to increase it. Instead of making all the decisions, you give choices to other people, setting them up to make good decisions themselves. Your team gains responsibility for almost everything that you, the leader, used to own.

You invest in others more as a mentor than as a manager. You pay attention to how people are doing and aim to maximize their impact. You're an ambassador or champion for your team. You always have time for people and are never too busy with your own tasks.

An empowered team is like an intelligent machine, and your role is to monitor, tweak, and improve the machine so it's always running well. That's a weird comparison, so let me put it another way.

Let's say a leader is like being a gardener. You can plant the seeds and then walk away, but that won't produce the best possible garden. Some types of fruit will do fine, but most need attention from a gardener.

If there isn't enough rainfall, a gardener waters the plants. If bugs or animals are attacking the plants, the gardener steps in. Weeds can spring up, which the gardener removes. These aren't glorious tasks, but they help the plants thrive. That's what a leader is like to the empowered team: The leader creates the best conditions for the seeds to thrive. (Can we just pretend for a minute that I didn't steal this phrase?)

The point I'm making is that there is still a role for a leader with an empowered team. Some people think empowerment is a one-time action to hand over Authority and walk away. But that only works if the variables stay the same, which will never be the case when dealing with constantly changing human beings and circumstances. Empowerment is the initial setup, and leadership is the ongoing support.

If I empower and then walk away, I abdicate my leadership and leave a big void. Have you ever heard people complain about not being appreciated, working too hard, always doing things they hate, and so on? Leadership that is consistently focused on others makes all the difference with those things.

The emphasis you place on leadership comes down to how much you want to realize the benefits of empowerment: maximized potential and growth. There must be constant leadership to see the best results. If a leader is supporting the team and helping people reach their full potential, the team will thrive all the more, positioning the company for growth.

If you empower the people on your team and then continue to help them grow, you're going to realize tremendous benefit. And think about what would happen if you develop other leaders. And then imagine if those leaders went and developed other leaders. That's the exponential impact that happens when you remove the dependency on yourself.

YOUR NEW JOB

Before we move on, I have something important to ask. After hearing about this leader role, do you want it? I know you probably want the benefits of an empowered team, but do you want your leadership focus to be about investing in others?

I once met with a successful company founder who said he wanted to get out of his business because of "people issues," as he called them. He had more employees than he could personally manage, and the problems kept piling up. Staff members weren't measuring up to his expectations, he constantly felt he had to follow up on outstanding items, and no one seemed to be able to make decisions without him.

However, his situation is not what I mean when I talk about supporting your team. Like so many other business owners, he felt trapped, having to micromanage every detail. I wondered whether he would still want to sell his business if he lead an empowered team.

I personally struggled to adjust to this new leader role, and often wondered whether I wanted my old job back. At times I wanted to go back to hiding in my office and making all the decisions. But eventually those moments were overshadowed by the fulfillment of setting up other people for success and becoming free from the day-to-day details.

Since this approach to leadership is so different, you'll also need different skills, which you may have to develop. (Remember Ability matters for your role too.) Leaders require emotional intelligence, such as being perceptive and caring. It also requires great communication skills, especially when it comes to sharing clear Context. I lacked these skills at first, so hopefully I can share something in the following chapters that will help you in the same way it helped me.

Later on we're going to learn more about how to support your team and to generate more growth. But first we need to deal with something that can be a showstopper for managers trying to be leaders: insecurity.

SUMMARY

- Being a leader by title is very different than being a leader by role.

- Managers make the decisions, solve the problems, and tell people what to do, but leaders of empowered teams avoid those things.

- A leader plays a supporting role and makes their team the hero, elevating others to thrive.

- As a leader, you should create the conditions for your team to succeed.

- Empowerment is the initial set-up phase and leadership is the ongoing support.

- Emphasis placed on good leadership directly affects the benefits of empowerment: maximized potential and growth.

- When you focus on investing in other people, you can have exponential impact.

- Managers contemplating this type of leadership should seriously consider if this is a role they want.

- The skillset of a leader is important to develop, including emotional intelligence and communication skills.

Ask yourself: Am I a leader or a manager most of the time? What am I doing right now to support my team and make them the hero?

- EIGHT -

CONFIDENT HUMILITY

I have very few memories from high school, and even fewer fond ones. I probably tried to push most of that phase of life out of my mind to be honest. However, I do have a vivid memory of this one guy who sat in the back seat of the school bus. Let's call him Tyrone. He was a huge bully who controlled the bus.

He was already there when I boarded every day, sitting at the back of the bus with his bully posse, a group of kids who enabled his brutish behavior. When people got on, he would often yell out insults while the posse laughed and spurred him on. Or he'd randomly throw stuff at people who wouldn't dare react lest something worse happen. He had the whole bus paralyzed in fear. He was like a tyrant ruling over his kingdom.

One time he yelled, "There's the Jesus boy," at me, presumably because my dad was a pastor. It was a silly phrase and more of a compliment than an insult, but it still bothered me. I was low on confidence back then, so having the attention of the entire bus was about the worst thing I could imagine. Although Tyrone did some damage to me, he was far less kind to others.

The bus driver got the brunt of Tyrone's antics. Let's call her Gail. To this day, I feel sick when I think of how she was treated.

She was a nice lady, maybe in her late forties or early fifties. Her face was withered and tired, as if she had a tough life, and her raspy voice hinted at a cigarette addiction that got the best of her. But Tyrone showed her no mercy, wearing her out day after day. It was almost like seeing a parent crack under pressure when dealing with an out-of-control toddler who is running around throwing things and hurting other kids. Tyrone would push Gail until she would lose it.

Gail would typically put on a kid-friendly radio station at a moderate volume, but on most days, Tyrone would yell, "Turn on Kool FM, Gail!" which was a radio station that was edgy and too controversial for teenagers to listen to at the time.

Gail would shake her head, as if she was bothered that a kid was calling the shots for her. Or maybe she knew she could get in trouble for putting *that* station on. But she still complied.

The kids on the bus knew what was coming next: "Turn it up, Gail!" Tyrone wasn't happy until he had reached the furthest limits of what he could get away with. He wanted to see just how close he could get to the cliff without falling off. It probably gave him a high in some weird way.

I remember one song that had the dirtiest lyrics, at least by the standards of the mid-nineties. It was called "Let's Talk about Sex." (That's right; it had the word "sex" in the title. Don't look it up, as it's about the cheesiest song in the world.) When that song came on, without fail Tyrone would yell out multiple times, "Turn it up, Gail!" followed by laughter from the bully posse. You could feel the tension. Gail knew she shouldn't turn up the volume on *that* song.

Then Tyrone stood up from his throne in the back seat and started walking to the front of the bus, with a cigarette hanging off his ear, as if to display his dominance. He grabbed the volume button and cranked it up.

What happened next was hard to watch back then, and it's even harder to tell now. Gail completely lost it. She pulled off the road, stood up, and started walking toward the back of the bus. Her face was beet red. She yelled at Tyrone at the top of her tired lungs, exploding with anger and emotional devastation. She was totally out of control.

As she walked back to her seat, I could tell she was fighting back tears. The bus was silent. Everyone was in complete shock. Tyrone and his posse were still snickering and whispering, but the mood had shifted.

I didn't see Gail for a while after that, and I wondered what had happened to her. Did she have a breakdown? Did she get in trouble for yelling at Tyrone? Eventually she came back, quite withdrawn and subdued. Tyrone was a little quieter at first, but soon returned to his antics. And the cycle repeated.

We can likely agree that Tyrone's behavior was despicable. But I would encourage you to think twice before you judge, because you may be similar to Tyrone in subtle ways, and that might be holding you back as a leader.

NO MORE SUPERHERO CAPE

We now need to cover a topic that you probably won't want to talk about (it isn't sex, by the way). This chapter is likely to be unpopular, but everything we're trying to achieve is in vain without this piece. I want to cover a key mindset shift that is essential to remove some potentially massive limitations. Without addressing this topic, you will likely fall short in the leader role. Are you ready?

Before learning about empowerment in the first section, we needed a critical mindset change: assuming success instead of failure. Hopefully you are no longer thinking, "Only I can be the best." But before we move forward with how to lead, you must also stop thinking, "I *want to* be the best." Perhaps you have gotten over thinking people on your team aren't as great as you, but you must also stop worrying about them overshadowing you. That's the mindset we now have to overcome.

To take on this leader role, you have to take off the superhero cape you've been wearing. You may be quite fond of the cape—how it feels, how it looks, and how people look at you when you have it on. It may be the source of your whole identity. But to be this type of leader you need to change from being a hero to having a supporting role, from having the spotlight shining on you to shining it on others, and from pursuing your own successes to setting others up for success.

This transition is similar to a pro athlete who retires from playing and becomes a coach. One day, massive stadiums of people are chanting his name, and the next he's standing on the sidelines with a potbelly and a bald head supporting the players. People were cheering for him, and now he is the one cheering. His ego takes a huge hit. That can't be easy for an athlete, and it likely won't be easy for you either.

You have to sincerely want others to be better than you are to see your team rise above you. That's tough for most people though. Even the smallest trace of insecurity will get in the way.

Insecurity is being uncertain about your own value. It's protecting your own superiority, guarding your own position, and constantly trying to elevate yourself.

I think bullies like Tyrone scream insecurity. Something has gone awry for people like that, and they feel the need to bring others down to feel better about themselves. They sit at the back of the bus to try to maintain a position of power. But empowerment is about delegating power, not wielding it over people.

THE B WORD

Leaders manifest insecurity in many ways. One way is with the term "boss." Maybe this is just a pet peeve of mine, but I don't like the word. Recently I was out with some friends, including someone from work, and I was introduced as his boss. Call me a colleague, a guy, or a friend—anything but the boss. The word carries an air of superiority to me.

I've noticed that kids love to use the B word too, which kills me. They'll say, "You're not the boss of me," or, "Mommy is the boss, not you" (said to a sibling; never to me, of course).

I think that if you crave being called boss, that's a problem. We all know that being bossy isn't desirable, so how does dropping the y and turning it into a noun make it okay? When someone uses the word, the intent may be to indicate positional authority, but to me the word carries too much baggage.

Here are some questions you can ask yourself to see whether you have traces of insecurity:

- Are you jealous when someone does something impressive?
- Do you feel threatened around other leaders who are younger and may seem ahead of you?
- Do you always have to be, or at least look, right?
- Are you bothered when other people talk more than you do in a meeting or conversation?
- Does it bother you if you are excluded from key conversations?
- Do you ever feel threatened in your position and try to protect it?
- Do you always make sure you're fully taken care of before helping others?
- Do you think of the organization as only yours?
- Do you avoid the phrase "I was wrong" at all costs?

When I started to transition from being a hero to having a supporting role, I wanted to make space for others to contribute in meetings, but I had trouble adjusting to getting less attention. It wasn't natural at first to give public credit to others, especially when it wasn't reciprocated. And the first few times the team said they didn't need me to help with a client call felt strange to me.

There was a moment in my empowerment journey when I suddenly ran out of things to do; things that made me feel like I'd accomplished something at the end of the day. One day I was driving home from work, and I couldn't think of a single task or project I'd accomplished on my own that day. Sure, I had helped others, and the business was moving forward better than ever, but I couldn't feel proud about any tangible thing that I had done personally. That left me feeling a little insecure.

Then there was the time I got a serious concussion and was stuck in a dark room for two weeks. It was as if I had fallen off the face of the earth and become totally unavailable. You might think I went back to work to a flurry of urgent questions and issues, but you'd be wrong. I walked in and everything was peaceful and under control. The thought crossed my mind that if things ran this smoothly when I had disappeared for two weeks, what exactly was I needed for?

BIG FAT BACKHOES

Insecurity comes in various forms and degrees. But in all cases, it will limit you and the people around you. When your focus is on elevating yourself, the natural by-product is to hold other people back.

Being held back is almost like getting stuck behind a backhoe on a single-lane highway. If the backhoe doesn't pull off the road to let you pass, it will keep you from reaching your top speed. Insecure leaders are driving big fat backhoes every day, and everyone else has to slow down behind them. Is that what you want to be—a big fat backhoe? I think not. (I should be an inspirational speaker.)

Remember, giving Authority to people is like giving someone a license to drive. Not giving authority to your team requires you to drive everyone around in your car. That is the cap—the number of people you can drive around in a day. But once you give people their licenses and let them have the driver's seat, you can still cap progress by driving in front of them. Leaders sometimes empower people but require everyone to stay behind them. Maybe your team has faster cars or are more familiar with a certain road, but they have to slow down for you. But aren't you all on the same team?

Consider what this behavior does to the potential of your team. Are you okay being the ceiling that no one can surpass? Do you want your organization's growth to be limited by your personal best?

HUMILITY IS COMPLICATED

Here's a deep question for you: Where do you get your value?

Do you get it from being in the spotlight? Do you think your insecurity is holding other people back, even in a small way?

If so, what are you supposed to do? I've read a lot about the topic, and some professionals say you should trace your insecurity back to the source to figure out exactly where it comes from. Apparently, it's often from a past experience. But this kind of psychological analysis is way outside my lane and not what I want to cover here.

A great start to dealing with insecurity is just to be aware of the limitation. Admit it. Say with me out loud, "My insecurity is a problem." Okay, I didn't think you would actually do it, but it was worth a shot. (Without the proper Context, people around you could think you're a little weird.) If you're aware that you have even traces of insecurity, you can fight it.

On that note, an empowering leader, you'll need to pursue a key trait: A true leader needs to be confidently humble. I understand that sounds like an oxymoron, so let me explain.

Humility is a complicated word that many people don't understand. Entrepreneurs or big-shot execs can see it as a negative, as if it equates with being small or showing weakness. They see it as not being able to have pride in what they do. I'm not saying you can't take pride in your work. Being pleased with your accomplishments is great. But demanding that you are the greatest is the wrong type of pride.

Humility is having a modest view of your own importance. It's seeing the team's importance as the same or greater than your own (not less). It's about how you see yourself with respect to others.

But I'm proposing *confident* humility. What is that? Confidence is the feeling you have when you are good at something. It's knowing you have value. I was missing this type of confidence on the bus with Tyrone. My humility was almost self-deprecating, which isn't the idea.

People with confident humility are people who thrive when they elevate others. They are people who see immense value in the people around them and are secure enough to help them excel. Those with confident humility stand up against injustice and ensure everyone has equal opportunity to succeed.

A leader who is confidently humble wants to help people become better than they are. That takes real character. There's no room for insecurity. With confident humility, you won't insist on being the best at everything or getting all the glory, but you will want others to shine and succeed. You can hold your head high while you serve others. This is the key to releasing the cap or the ceiling that can be imposed on a team.

BLAME YOURSELF

If you have confident humility and something goes wrong, you examine and blame yourself first. You think about what you missed or what more you could have done. Instead of deflecting and making excuses, you say the seamingly unspeakable phrase that is so powerful coming from a leader: "I was wrong."

A person with confident humility invites feedback and strives to improve. You try to learn from the people around you. You ask people: Where do you think we could improve? Or where do you think *I* could improve?

I once asked a few people on my team an impromptu question during some one-on-one meetings: "If you were the CEO, what would you do differently?"

It was funny to watch some of them squirm in their seats. They wondered whether my question was okay to discuss directly with me. But after some awkward silence, many offered great feedback. That type of a vulnerable question increases unity and buy-in of a team.

With confident humility, you're fine to let other people make important decisions or manage key meetings without you. You can surround yourself with very talented people—people who are better than you at many things. And you want them to do what they do best.

AN INTERESTING CONTRADICTION

The idea of confident humility, for some leaders, could sound like a demotion. But there is an interesting contradiction that ends up happening.

As counterintuitive as it might seem, if you humble yourself for the greater good of the team, real growth occurs. The more you value others over yourself, the more your influence and impact grows.

But here's the catch. You have to sincerely value others, and not just for what you get out of it. If you focus on your own growth, you can taint the authenticity of the humility. But if you really care about helping people succeed and thrive, and if you devote your attention to that more than to your own situation, then the magic happens. As you stop worrying about your own aspirations, the rest falls into place.

Instead of basing your value on building a great business and being in the spotlight, what if you based your value on seeing others succeed, in building great people, and in helping others thrive? The results of that would be massive. You will achieve exponential impact, but it starts with confidently humbling yourself. Are you down?

SERVE, NOT SERVED

I've got an example of confident humility, but I should warn you that it's a little controversial. When I think of a leader who was confidently humble, I think of Jesus. Don't worry, it doesn't make any difference whether you believe he's God or not for this illustration. In some ways, the story of Jesus is more impressive if you're not a Christian. (Now I'm offending all possible audiences.)

What I mean by impressive is that you probably know Jesus's name, and it's been over two thousand years since he was on Earth. Even if his name is just the word you yell when you stub your toe, you still know it. That puts Jesus in an elite category of leaders who have lasted for centuries. It makes me curious about how he pulled this off from an empowerment perspective.

From what the Bible says, Jesus worked with his team (called disciples) for only three years. He didn't even have to travel that far to share his cause. His game plan was to empower other people to spread the message.

In my opinion, he was the Context master. He constantly spoke in parables, which were analogies and stories, and he asked questions to help people understand. He got people thinking rather than telling them how to think, which seemed to annoy the religious leaders of that time. His goal seemed to be to redefine a controlling system to be more about authentic love and matters of the heart.

He saw potential in everyone he encountered and always assumed success. He even gave away Authority and told people they would do greater things than he did, which sounds pretty secure to me. The Bible says that Jesus came "not to be served but to serve others" (Mark 10:45 NLT). At one point, he washed the feet of his disciples. Most of the people I work with shower every day and wear clean socks and shoes, but I wouldn't consider doing that.

The Bible also says, "In humility value others above yourselves, not looking to your own interests but each of you to the interests of the others" (Philippians 2:3-4 NIV). That sums up confidently humble leadership perfectly.

It's amazing to see someone who has tremendous power deciding to use that power to help others—someone with a big title choosing a role of service. That's the model for leadership that seems to be so uncommon these days. Centuries later, we still hear Jesus' name. This makes me wonder if there's something to this humble way of leading.

With that in mind, we're ready to figure out where we are going to find the time to help people. I'm guessing you don't have enough time for your own stuff, let alone considering others.

SUMMARY

- Leaders must stop worrying about their teams overshadowing them.

- It's possible to empower people but not allow them to get ahead of you (which is often done without even realizing it).

- Empowerment is about delegating power, not wielding it over people.

- It can be a difficult adjustment to go from being the hero to playing a supporting role.

- Insecurity can be a major limitation; if you are uncertain about your own value, then you will try to ensure you are superior.

- Insecurity limits the success of the people around you.

- If your focus is to elevate yourself, the natural by-product is to hold others back.

- You have to fight insecurity, to elevate others above yourself.

- Leaders with confident humility are secure enough to focus on helping others succeed.

- Confident humility means being open to feedback, comfortable with fewer people depending on them, and able to promote others.

- For the greatest success, you must genuinely want your team to rise above you.

- You must redefine where you find your value to focus on elevating others.

- Confident humility is a contradiction—it ends up elevating the entire team.

Ask yourself: In what ways am I insecure as a leader? How has this held me and my team back?

- NINE -

GAIN MARGIN

Some people think that being busy equates to being important, as if busyness were a measure for success.

I once asked a friend, who constantly seems busy, to get together for coffee. The following conversation happened in mid-March (that detail matters).

I started with an upbeat tone. "Yo, dude, we need to get together for coffee—it's been too long!"

He messaged back, all business. "Totally. I have May 29 at 10:15 a.m.?"

That was two-and-a-half months later! Months, not weeks. A whole change of seasons from winter to spring. I'm not even sure my calendar reaches that far in the future. Plus he was booking in fifteen-minute increments, like I was being slotted in for my semiannual cleaning at the dentist.

I wrote back jokingly. "I'm pretty booked up that day, but I can probably make it work if we do 10:23 to 11:17 a.m.—cool?" (Unfortunately, he didn't think my joke was as clever as I thought it was.)

DIGGING MY WAY OUT

To me, it's annoying when people brag about the number of emails they get. "Oh man, I just got a hundred emails while I was at lunch." Or try being with someone who has his or her phone set to maximum volume for email alerts so everyone knows who the bigshot is.

If your email alert has gone off more than once while reading the last paragraph, turn the dumb thing off. Seriously. If you get that much activity and you already look at your phone a hundred times a minute, the alert is pointless, other than showing off to people of course.

Then there are the people who announce they're unavailable by using the phrase "digging my way out." For example, "I've been away from my desk for a couple of hours, so I have to dig my way out before we can talk." For me the phrase invokes a mental picture that doesn't jive with a successful business leader.

A person who is extremely busy is probably someone who hasn't empowered people. The person is ineffective and a bottleneck. Do you really want to advertise that to everyone?

Busyness is the enemy of impact. Time spent on tasks means time not spent with your team. Being busy often means being distracted from what you should be doing: investing in people.

This is a major paradigm shift for most leaders, however. It's very foreign from the accepted norm.

If someone wants to book some time with you and asks what a certain day looks like in the near future, try this response: "I've got nothing that day—I'm completely free!" Then watch for the confused or concerned look that says, "Poor guy isn't doing so well. The market must have taken a turn. We should pray for him." When I say this, most people think I'm lying.

They can't imagine that I'm not actually as busy as they are.

I joke about it now, but busyness was all I knew for years, so I can relate. Let me make the case for how I became convinced that a leader shouldn't be busy. (Now is a great time to take a break to catch up on your bulging email inbox while you still think that matters.)

PRIVATE JETS AND RARE CIGARS

The first leader I'd ever met who didn't seem insanely busy was a legendary businessman named Marco. Now in his late forties, he's a driven, charismatic guy who was highly successful at a very young age. When I met him, he had just stepped down from his position as the youngest president of a huge company where he led thousands of employees and brought in over $1 billion in revenue. Thus, I assumed he knew what he was doing.

He also had epic stories about flying on private jets to tropical islands for quick meetings, or tracking down rare cigars to help close gazillion-dollar deals. The point is, he's legendary. A mutual friend introduced me to Marco, and he agreed to coach me for a little while.

A few years ago, I had the chance to go on a short business trip with him. A company was interested in buying mine, but I had the feeling they thought I was an innocent child who could be convinced to trade my company for some free passes to Disneyland. Enter Marco—private jet, exotic cigar, deal-closer Marco. He had the effect of making me look way more legit than I actually was, which I quite enjoyed.

Marco and I went to meet the executives that wanted to buy my company at an expensive hotel in downtown New Orleans. A lady met us in the lobby and escorted us up to the penthouse suite before leaving us with the CEO and his entourage. They started the conversation with an air of superiority, looking mainly at me. I could sense that Marco was getting ready to pounce. Then for the rest of the meeting, he proceeded to dominate the group of older businessmen while I looked on in delight. It was like watching an Olympic event where you can't believe the competitors are normal people like you and me.

It was one of the best learning experiences of my life. However, it wasn't Marco's ability to dominate the business transaction that made the biggest impact on me.

During the entire day of traveling with Marco, he looked at his phone maybe two or three times—total. Back then, if I looked at my phone that many times in a single minute, I was probably in the bathroom, or I'd dropped the phone between the seats in the car, in which case I was freaking out trying to pull it free.

During our trip, I thought Marco was wasting time by not using his phone very much. It seemed to me that he could have been more productive while traveling. But I had trouble reconciling that thought with the tremendous success he's had. How could such an impressive guy be sitting here so peacefully without constant calls and messages constantly coming in?

Instead, Marco was fully present in our conversations. He was 100 percent with me. He also used his brain just to *think*. He had mental space to come up with ideas, and to dream.

At the time, I only noticed this stuff because I didn't think it made any sense. It was out of place so it caught my eye, in the same way that you might notice a chimpanzee riding the subway.

A CONSTANT STREAM OF ISSUES

Although that trip with Marco challenged the stereotype I had of what a successful leader looked like, I didn't immediately change my ways. I had a cocky attitude and thought I was more productive or progressive by capitalizing on every spare second I had.

Gradually, I began to reconsider what it means to not be busy. Let me share what I learned. I am not suggesting that you should do absolutely nothing. What I'm advocating for is limiting your obligations. An obligation is something you are bound to do. The word conveys the idea of imprisonment. It's a commitment or a duty. An obligation naturally comes with owning something or having responsibility.

If you're a parent, have you ever noticed how different it is being around kids when yours aren't around? There's a different feeling of responsibility. I was on a flight recently when a baby girl acted up. She started crying and trying to climb out of her mom's arms. Meanwhile, I sat there peacefully writing my notes and having a snack as if nothing was happening.

My blood pressure didn't even rise, because I had no responsibility or obligation.

Then the baby threw her bottle, and some milk squirted all over the floor and on my pant leg. Again, the mess wasn't my problem. But I certainly had the time and flexibility to help out, so I did. I picked up the bottle and handed it to the mom with a smile. I could make the choice to help out if I wanted to. My experience would have been very different if I had been the parent.

(As an aside, I certainly wondered what was in the bottle. Would I be sitting for the rest of the ten-hour flight with breast milk on my leg? I believe that was a first for me. But it's not at all the point.)

If you lead a customer-support department and a client escalates a major issue, then you'll drop everything to handle it. It's like *your* kid threw a bottle of breast milk on the client, and you are responsible to clean things up and apologize.

You may have a constant stream of issues (no pun intended) that come up from various areas, but that probably means you have responsibility for more than you should. When you have an obligation to act, that means you have some form of ownership. And that's what we're trying to limit.

By contrast, a big problem emerged the other day at work, and guess what I did? Nothing. Okay, not nothing. I heard some people scrambling, so I walked over to ask what was up and whether they needed help. They gave me a brief update and said they had it taken care of. So, I went back to my office and ate an apple. I wasn't the owner, and the obligation wasn't on me.

An empowering leader's goal is to have less work that you alone must do—work that only gets done with your involvement. The show should go on with or without you.

You add tremendous value when you're present, but you don't *have* to be present. The choice is yours of when and how you want to add value. This means you are being proactive, not reactive.

For example, I'm often an optional attendee at meetings that I used to run. When I attend, I try to be helpful and to make a contribution. But if something else comes up, I can just skip it. The success of the meeting doesn't depend on me. And I usually don't walk away with a list of actions when I leave.

I like to call this extra space in the day "margin." Margin on a page is the space that is intentionally left blank. Some people talk about financial margin, which is a little buffer that helps them traverse unforeseen hardships. Margin with time is having that same buffer for whatever may come up.

CREATING THE NECESSARY SPACE

So that's what I mean by being less busy. The question is: Why does it matter so much?

There are the obvious reasons, such as enjoying life a little more. People get so desensitized about being busy that they almost don't think about what the alternative would be like. But as one who has experienced both sides, I can tell you that leaders who empower their teams are much better off. There's no comparison. It's far less stressful to not be so busy, which must be better for your health. But being happy and healthy are really just side benefits of my main point.

The key reason to be less busy is to create the necessary space that's needed to invest in the people around you.

Remember that exponential impact happens through other people—people whom you support and inspire. And supporting people is less predictable compared to working on your own tasks.

If you're constantly busy, there's no way to provide the kind of leadership that your team needs. It's just not going to happen. There will always be something else to do. This abdication of leadership will be felt, and you can say good-bye to seeing the uncapped growth that occurs when people reach their potential.

This chapter is a primer intended to prepare you for the role that I'm going to outline in the next few chapters. You must actually have the time to reinforce people's Authority, invest in their growth, and advance toward your goals. The success of empowerment depends on you having margin.

A FULL PLATE

I struggle with the balance of leading versus doing; that is, supporting others versus doing work of my own. I have a lot of trouble switching between the two mindsets.

After I eat supper, I need everything to be put away before I can enjoy the evening. If I were to start reading a book with dishes still in the sink, I would hear the dirty pots and pans calling my name. If I tried to push my way through the book with brute force, I wouldn't enjoy it. Eventually I'd have to put it down and clean things up before I continued reading.

That's the feeling of having work waiting for you. If you're like me, you're not going to mingle with your team and look for opportunities to mentor or help them while your plate is full (figuratively speaking). You're going to work through the task list and then help people. It's like putting on your airplane oxygen mask before assisting other passengers. If you force yourself to put the work aside, you will constantly be thinking, "When can this be over so I can stop wasting my time and go complete my important tasks?"

Let's assume for a second that you get through your work (which is often not the case). There's still another problem. Your brain has to make a big mental shift from task-based work to a completely different mindset: being creative and strategic by interacting with and investing in people. Once you get sucked into tasks, it's hard to get out, both physically and mentally.

At home, some nights it can feel like there is a lot of work to do, such as taking out the garbage or dealing with the kids' messes. (I know that they should be empowered to clean up their own messes, but I'm still working on applying this empowerment stuff at home.) After doing all these tasks, I put aside productivity and instead end up crashing onto the couch to watch TV, and I don't mean an educational documentary. That's the problem with focusing on your own tasks first—you may not come out on the other side as the visionary others-focused leader that people need.

A VICIOUS CYCLE

Apparently science has shown that there is something in the brain that makes it hard for us to switch from transactional to transformational stuff, or from being reactive to proactive. So, I should do the proactive stuff, such as a brainstorming session, before taking care of my emails. But now we're back to the last point—I hear the emails calling my name. It's a vicious cycle.

My solution was a little extreme. I decided to get insane about not having ownership over anything. It started out as a joke; I told my senior team that my new goal was to do sweet nothing. But as I started to head in that direction, I realized that it actually made a lot of sense. If I was responsible for nothing, then my whole job was to make sure everyone else accomplished their responsibilities with no distractions.

I prefer the senior-most leader (by title) committing to a full-time supportive leadership-role, or as close to that as possible. You can decide where to draw the line. It will depend on your long-term goals, such as what you want your involvement to look like and your vision for expansion. My goal was growth and getting out of the day-to-day details, so I was pretty aggressive with my time choices.

Your desired margin also depends on the stage you're at with empowerment. I met a guy recently who founded a charity and was very interested in learning how to empower his team. He certainly had a huge need. During our meeting, he took a bunch of notes and was excited to start implementing the framework when he left.

But he told me a few days later that all the excitement died the moment he got into his car and saw the work that was piling up. He couldn't even get started due to his busyness, so he quit trying. Gaining margin was really just the first step in his empowerment journey. I suggested that he might have to make some tough choices for a season, to do less as an organization, in order to gain control of his time.

You may need to consider scaling back your vision, at least temporarily. Maybe you have five products that could be reduced to four. Maybe you need to scale back some initiatives, such as delaying a building project or a marketing overhaul.

Or you could also consider reviewing your expectations for excellence. Perhaps your current standard of excellence is not realistic given your bandwidth. How's that for advice? Be more mediocre. Maybe you're building a new product that is overly fancy. If so, get less fancy. Maybe you are over the top in customer service. Back that up just a pinch.

It might seem unthinkable to scale back, but this is a temporary measure to gain margin, empower your team, and see sustainable impact and growth. The alternative is to keep doing what you're doing until you burn out and the team leaves you. At least you'll go out on a high note, right?

I'm trying to put this decision in perspective. This is about positioning for the future. In no time, you can pick up where you left off and get back to your former glory (and beyond) once you can handle it.

There's one other factor to consider when deciding your target margin percentage. You may be passionate about and want to continue in certain roles. That's okay as long as you don't let this be your excuse to keep doing every single thing that comes along. You must have sufficient time to lead your team.

GET YOUR GUARD UP

Regardless of your goals, and regardless of your ability to juggle leading and doing, you could probably stand to be less busy. So, you have to assess what to do with your time and what to allow into your world.

This process won't be easy. For every single thing you do, you have to ask: Can I hand this off? Should I be involved in this? Is this worth taking me away from time as a leader? Who could own this? You have to be ruthless to get the margin you need. You may even need someone to hold you accountable or to help push you to make tough decisions.

As you assess each task, you'll likely struggle to let go. Getting used to the mindset that others can and should do what you do is not easy.

When I have time-assessment conversations with people, I might start by asking about the types of emails they get. As they open their inbox, I often see hundreds or thousands of unread messages. I take a deep breath and press on into a conversation that usually goes something like this.

"Okay, show me just the most recent couple of emails," I say.

"Here's one from today. I'm copied on a response to TechCo about a meeting that's coming up. Sally sent it—our CFO. That's important for sure." The defensive tone starts before I've even said anything, which tells me I'm likely onto something.

I used to be quick to give opinions, but I've learned that real change tends to happen when I simply ask questions and guide the conversation to help people come to realizations on their own. Many questions I ask involve the word "why." So, I ask, "Tell me why you're included in that email exchange."

The person says, "I need to know the meeting is booked, first of all. It's a big one, since we're setting up a new invoicing solution that we've launched to help our clients better manage . . ."

I try to politely interrupt the unnecessary details. "So that's the reason—to know the meeting is being scheduled?"

The person senses the need to add more justification. "Oh, I almost forgot. What if Sam misses the response? I can't let this one slip between the cracks."

"Okay, so you want to ensure a meeting has been scheduled," I say, to confirm that I'm not missing the point. "Are you the only one who can do this?"

We go through another email or two. Someone on the team is asking for a Friday off. I repeat a similar series of questions. Then the person I'm talking to objects with a crazy justification that he or she is the only one in the universe who can make that kind of serious judgment call to review leave requests. I ask the person if it would be possible to hand off the requests to another team member, but still get a weekly report, or to only be brought in for unusual circumstances. The person might write down the idea for "future consideration," and we move on.

Then we look at the person's calendar. "I've got a sales review meeting at nine, a client issues meeting at ten, and an office lease meeting at eleven."

I interrupt as I start to lose my cool. "Are you the one leading all these meetings?" I ask, to which the answer is inevitably yes.

Then we transition to tasks. "Okay, how about your to-do list? What do we have?"

"Let me see. It's kind of out of control right now. It's been a hectic few weeks, and I'm still digging my way out!" the person says as if it's a joke—some kind of sick, twisted, humorless joke. "All righty, here we go. I've got to prepare a sales report for the board, plus a status update for the support team . . ." The person pauses and then continues. "Oh, wait a second . . . I already emailed part of that, so I just need to follow up and make sure they have it. After that, I have to get back to one of our clients about a question."

Meanwhile, I'm looking awkwardly at the ceiling, waiting for the person to realize I am still sitting there. This is typical of how these conversations go.

Despite the difficulties of this process, it can be a great exercise—if you're actually willing to consider changes.

CUTTING AND SLASHING

Another way to free your schedule is to keep a journal of how you're spending your time. You'll have to be honest with yourself if you want it to be effective. You could categorize your time by what you're obligated to do versus things you could choose to do. Then go through each of the obligations one by one to see whether you can delegate some (or all) of them.

Your log could say things like "brought into x" or "had urgent y come up" or "z took way longer than expected." The point is to get your activities on paper so you can know where your time is going and be able to track your margin percentage as you make improvements.

Then start cutting and slashing. (It's as violent as it sounds.) Examine everything to see what should remain and what can be delegated to an empowered person. You have to have the stomach for this kind of cutting—it's not for the weak.

It's like convincing a hoarder to throw away a bunch of stuff. I used to struggle with getting rid of things, and I would stress over each item while trying to make the case that it would be needed in the future. Then even if I finally agreed to let it go, I'd reminisce about where the item was purchased, or the good times we had together. Then I'd smell it and hold it. You get the idea—it's a painful process.

Once you get the margin you want, you can't let your guard down or let busyness creep back in. Often I find myself getting distracted with my own work. Before I know it, I'm busy again. I revert back to not having enough time for the leader role.

To guard against this, I try to track my time on an ongoing basis, just to know I've got the margin I want and need. My senior team discusses this quite often to hold each other accountable. We don't want to be recovering hoarders who starts hoarding again with all the empty space.

By now we should have the right mindset to be leaders and the time to do what's required. I know it's taken a while to get here, so thanks for your patience. Now let's learn exactly what a leader does.

SUMMARY

- Being busy isn't a measure of success; instead, it shows a lack of being a leader with an empowered team.

- Busyness can be the enemy of impact, since time on tasks means time away from your team.

- Seeking to be less busy is a big paradigm shift, a foreign concept to the accepted norm.

- Leaders should limit obligations, the things you are obligated to do.

- Leaders should be in a position to be proactive with time, not reactive, with the choice of when and where to add value.

- Having margin ensures there is time for investing in people, which greatly affects the success of empowerment.

- Balancing tasks and mentoring is mentally difficult; it's not easy to concentrate on others when distracted with your own work.

- A senior leader should consider no owned roles other than the leader role, depending on long-term goals and personal interest.

- If you have no time, tough choices may be necessary, such as temporarily scaling back your vision or expectations for excellence; however, this is necessary for empowering more people.

- Assess everything you do by looking at emails, tasks, and calendar entries; keep a journal to track your time, and then be aggressive to meet your target margin percentage.

Ask yourself: Do I have enough margin to be an effective leader? What changes should I consider making?

- TEN -

REINFORCE EMPOWERMENT

There's a big misconception out there in the universe when it comes to empowerment and delegation. People often think it's all about the initial handoff, which is the part I covered in the first section of the book. Although the way you delegate is crucial, it's only the first step.

The success of empowerment in the long term is determined more by what comes *after* you hand over control. Empowerment isn't an initiative that you emphasize for a time and then forget about. It's difficult to hand over the keys to someone, but it's almost harder to not be a backseat driver who is perpetually instructing, criticizing, and grabbing the wheel. With empowerment, you may still be in charge, but in certain areas you are no longer in direct control.

You may be handing off something that you used to do for decades. As you delegate your work, you're still brushing shoulders with the person every day. As the more experienced person with the important title, you are always watching. So, what you do around that person determines the long-term success of the transition.

To put that in perspective, you're basically taking a front-row seat at a performance you had done for years. You'll be shining the spotlight on your team, but that doesn't mean you won't be tempted to jump on stage, especially when you know it would be easier or faster for you to do it yourself. And the temptation is almost irresistible if someone on your team invites you to step in. I've had many cases where I sat through a call I used to make or a meeting I used to host. It killed me to stay quiet, and I failed at it many times.

For you to lead an empowered team, and for your team to stay empowered, you have to resist the temptation to retake control. Many people do a decent job of initially empowering, but keeping people empowered is the hardest part and is often done poorly.

You're probably going to need to replace some bad habits with some good ones. Natural behaviors need to be replaced with new unnatural ones. I've heard that it usually takes weeks to form a habit. That's a long time to be doing something you're not used to or comfortable with.

Perhaps you spent your whole life on the controlling end of the spectrum and suddenly you're handing out Authority to your team. Previously you could give an opinion on any topic at any time. You could snap your fingers and command something to be done. Now you must exercise restraint and inject yourself at the right times, and you're likely not used to this scenario.

As I made the transition from control to empowerment, it helped me to have a handful of empowerment principles to govern which actions I should take in any given situation. I worked for a *system* that guided my decisions, not my feelings or personal preferences. Whatever lined up with empowerment is what I would do. The next two chapters are substantially about this system, one that will keep the people around you empowered.

BECAUSE I SAID SO

You also can't overlook the people on your team, who are used to being controlled. You might think the change to empowerment will be met with celebration, as if you set your team free from prison. But empowerment is not always instantly adopted. I believe that slow adoption is often tied to the way parents answer questions with the word "why."

Kids seem to be born with a desire to understand the world around them. It's as if there is a natural skeptic in them. Or maybe it's just curiosity. The point is that they instinctively want Context. But instead of fostering this, many parents or authority figures discourage it.

A lot of kids ask their parents why questions, and the response is "because" with a period at the end, as if that's an answer.

"Why do I have to come here?"

"Because." That's not even a complete sentence, let alone an answer.

Or, "Why do I have to eat that?"

"Because I said so." Okay, now you're using more words, but it's equally useless an answer.

Let's think about this. You want your kids to grow up to be smart, successful, empowered people who can make great choices for themselves. Yet when they practically beg you to help them get there, you shut them down. I realize I probably need to calm down— obviously I'm passionate about this one.

My point is that through many parts of life, starting at childhood, messages can be sent that imply true understanding doesn't matter or isn't worth the time investment. And this continues through school and many jobs.

The real problem in not answering kids' why questions isn't that they'll lack information; it's that the kids will stop asking questions. They lose their will to fight for the Context they need to be empowered.

Without understanding, people have no choice but to follow instructions. And that means they can't be in positions to exercise ownership and take initiative. That makes for the ideal candidate to a controlling manager but not the new you.

Many people will not be used to an ownership culture where it's not only acceptable but encouraged to ask why, to be curious, and to demand understanding. There will be no step-by-step tasks; instead people will need to own objectives. Can you guess whose responsibility it is to make the culture shift? I'll give you a hint; it's not your team's.

THE CULTURE CURATOR

This chapter is about taking responsibility so that you and your team do the right things to make sure people stay empowered. A key role of a leader is to model and defend empowerment. You're the head cheerleader for empowerment. (It's up to you whether you want to carry around pom-poms.)

I have a friend who has the official title of Culture Curator. I've never said this to his face, but I think it's a funny title. I imagine his office as having a secret room hidden behind a sliding bookshelf. In the room I see endless shelves of big black metal pots filled to the brim with culture, lots and lots of culture.

He is the curator of said culture and pulls some out every now and then when it's needed. I see him also having secret ingredients up on a high shelf. (He'd need one of those tall sliding ladders to reach them, like those in a huge library.) He can mix the ingredients over a stove and *voilà,* more culture. Sometimes I picture him pulling down pots and staring at the culture, dreaming of what to do with it next.

Okay, that got off topic. The point I want to make is that any leader is a culture curator of sorts. This role is not something to delegate or outsource. A leader is responsible for setting the tone for culture at all times.

This role starts with talking about culture often, referencing core values when decisions are made, and teaching about desired behaviors. For example, in my company I started doing a weekly culture talk. This was a lesson or an interactive discussion about how we apply our values to what we're doing.

This role of instilling culture also involves making sure that the desired behaviors are shining through. Are people consistently representing what matters most? Are decisions being made that align with core values?

But what I want to focus on next is what you should do and not do around people who have already been empowered. You are responsible for ensuring each person on your team is empowered each day. In doing so, you'll set a great example for the behaviors that you want the team to replicate. It sounds like a lot of pressure, and it is.

THE POINTS SYSTEM

I believe every interaction you have in a day affects ownership. The pettiest details of how you interact with people matter. Either you reinforce people's ownership, or you steal it back for yourself.

I probably shouldn't use this comparison, but this reminds me of something I've told a couple of guys who were new to marriage (and only when my wife wasn't around). Some people say that a husband can get points for doing nice things, like five points for flowers or fifteen points for a spontaneous gift. (These values are subjective and don't necessarily apply to your situation.) On the other hand, points can be lost for messing up, but I'm not going to share examples here, as I don't believe that would be productive.

A lot of guys don't realize that husbands can never have more than zero points. Coming out even is the best you can ever aspire to. Despite the fact that every wrong move sends you spiraling into the negatives, a series of great moves doesn't make you soar into the positives.

Let me give you an example. Let's say my points are breakeven and I buy some flowers. Even though that technically represents five points, it still brings me from zero to, you guessed it, zero. You can't store up extra points for a rainy day like money in a bank. Let's say I make a really bad move and lose fifty points (not saying I've ever done anything *that* bad). Now the flowers points count again, but I've got a steep hill to climb to get back to zero.

I've seen the same rookie move so many times, when someone tries to bank up deposits, but it's all in vain. So innocent. So naïve. Rest assured that when you slip up, you're going down. (Am I right to assume every woman is now done reading the rest of this book?)

As a leader, let's say you have fifty good interactions with someone and then one bad one. The fifty interactions bring you to neutral, which is a fully empowered person. But the bad one brings you down. Oh, and I forgot to mention that bad interactions can count for double or triple the points—it just depends on the severity of the offense.

I'm obviously exaggerating, but my point is that you need to be deliberate to consistently do things that empower instead of control. I'm a fan of the word "deliberate" when it comes to leadership. It means something is done intentionally and consciously. If you have a plan going into interactions with people, you can be intentional about following the plan. And you can be open to feedback and self-assessment, which will help you be conscious of how you do each time. Good coaching can help, if you're open to it.

For starters, you have to know what each person on your team owns, and the Ability and Context that supports their Authority. Then you are your team's advocate, making sure that their Context and Authority remain strong. That is what I will cover in the next two chapters.

(If you happen to be still fuming about the points joke, please note that it was just that: a joke. No actual relationships were harmed in the making of this joke. In fact, I'm living the life right now with plus thirty or so points, subject to change of course.)

SUMMARY

- Delegating Authority initially is much easier than keeping people empowered in the long term.

- What you do around your team determines the success of empowerment.

- There is a constant temptation to return to being the controlling manager, so you must recognize this and fight against it.

- Your team may need help adjusting to empowerment and the need for understanding.

- The culture shift from controlling to empowering behaviors should be championed by the senior leader.

- A key part of the leader role is to model and defend empowerment.

- Every interaction you have with people matters.

- You must be deliberate (something done intentionally and consciously) to do things that empower instead of control.

- A leader must ensure the team's Context and Authority remains strong.

Ask yourself: Am I consistently setting the tone for a culture of empowerment? In what ways should I take more responsibility over culture?

- ELEVEN -

ENSURE CONTEXT

Since things change in an organization every day, sharing Context isn't just a one-time thing. We already discussed the importance of providing the Context needed for people to be empowered, but that's not the end. You have to make sure the person stays connected to the right information. Maintaining Context is about communication—making sure you put in the effort to communicate in effective ways. If you give people roles and then hold back information they need, they will be set up for failure.

SUMMERTIME TUXEDOS

Do you know what it's like to feel left out of a conversation? Think about what it's like when people are laughing at an inside joke and you're doing the fake-laughing thing while you decide whether you should ask what is so funny. If you ask, then you feel awkward for previously laughing at a joke you didn't even get. And if you don't ask, you'll forever be in the dark.

Obviously, it's no fun to be left out. But feelings aside, the lack of information places a limitation on you. You can't jump in with that perfectly timed witty comment since you have no idea what the joke is even about.

A few years ago, I was in a friend's wedding. There was a rehearsal the night before with an informal dress code, but one of the guys told an usher that it was a full dress rehearsal. So dressy he came.

I remember him walking down a long dirt road to the outdoor location in the hot summer sun dressed in his tuxedo. The rest of the guys (including me, I'll admit) were staked out away from view doing the best job we could to mute our laughter. While he was walking, I thought about how much effort he had put in to get ready and I felt bad. But I laughed. (And laughed.)

When we jumped out from our hidden location, in our shorts and tee-shirts, the usher's face was beet red. He tried to laugh, but it was a forced laughter, as if he knew this story was going down in history, and that if he blew up it would only be that much more legendary.

I realize in this story that the usher wasn't just left out of a joke; he *was* the joke. But this shows that it doesn't feel good to be left out of key information, and it prevents people from properly preparing and participating. That can make them feel like they are the joke.

CONSTANT COMMUNICATION

It might sound simple but maintaining Context starts with communication. As a leader, your job is to constantly keep people in the know. You must always be on the lookout for Context gaps that you can fill. You have to consistently consider the perspectives of others to ensure they know what they need to know. I'm not saying you've been laughing at the people on your team who are dressed in tuxedos, but you certainly need to step in if you see them reaching for their cummerbunds.

If someone's role changes, tell everyone. If there is a change to best practices for remote working, tell everyone. Are you changing the target market for sales? Tell everyone connected to sales (which is probably everyone). If you see someone struggling to understand something, use phrases like, "Here is some background information on this."

Good communication also applies to notices about future direction. A key part of sharing information is providing advanced notice.

One of my least favorite questions is, "Do you have a sec?" First of all, it's a rhetorical question. Everyone with a pulse has a sec. Give me some Context first and then I can answer the question. "I'm wondering whether I could have less than five minutes of your time for feedback on x." Now that's an empowering question. I'm now in a position to decide whether I indeed have a sec.

One common practice in organizations is to have last-minute, spontaneous meetings where no advance Context is provided. As a result, people can't prepare, which creates the feeling of being controlled. Under those circumstances, people can't bring their best. But this could all be fixed by remembering to communicate. It can be hard to get into the habit, but once you have it, it's actually an easy thing to do.

UNDERGROUND MEETINGS

In order for you to share information, you need to be inclusive and transparent. A controlling environment, on the other hand, is exclusive. Information is kept private and confidential. But if you restrict access to information, I believe you control your team.

Being inclusive didn't come naturally to me at first. For example, I liked exclusive gatherings of the leadership team. I enjoyed the top-secret conversations and private information during meetings for the elite few with the right security clearance.

Eventually I realized that the entire company could benefit from what was being shared in the leadership team's weekly underground meetings. It became clear that exclusive gatherings widened the

Context gap between the people on the inside and those on the outside.

I still remember the day I brought my proposal to the leadership team about opening up our meetings. Their expressions basically told me I was an idiot. To be fair, I thought I was an idiot too. But I was committed to following this framework at all costs, even when it wasn't natural or my preference. And this transition certainly was not my preference.

This change had a very positive impact on the entire company. Previously excluded people suddenly felt part of important discussions. This provided them with significant Context to give them a shot at growing and making better decisions. And (big shocker) there was almost nothing that was too confidential for the whole company to hear.

Sharing information with the entire team doesn't mean that you need to invite them to every meeting. That wouldn't be practical. But there should always be someone in the room who is responsible for communicating key updates to everyone who needs the information. Perhaps you could use a central communications system to share updates and allow access to reports and information, or maybe team leads take the time to have a daily huddle with their staff. Whatever method you use, make sure you share the information effectively.

HOLD NOTHING BACK

In addition to being inclusive, a leader should set the tone for being transparent as well. It's one thing to include people, but it's another level to be forthright and honest about what you're sharing. People value transparency at a human level. It also gives them deeper Context to thrive. But this concept tends to freak out many leaders.

I find that leaders often shut people out during times of transition or uncertainty. But in those cases, there are actually more reasons to share everything you can. Let's say a product launch isn't going well. If you shut people off from this information, you'll probably end up resorting to control to fix the situation. But if you bring people up to date, they are empowered to help solve the problem.

One time we were on the verge of losing a very important client and I naturally didn't want to tell people in our weekly all-team meeting. But we sided with empowerment and told everyone. I gave the status update, including the things I didn't understand and even how I felt about the whole thing. I held nothing back.

It was extremely well received, and our team had a great discussion about it. Some ideas came up, but it also generated a lot of unity. You might not always present exciting or happy news, which will require a lot of confident humility, but you have to share it.

There are obviously topics like salaries or personnel matters that must remain private, but you should share as much as you possibly can. Give people a shot at having access to what they want and need to grow and become more empowered.

Consider for yourself, have you shared everything needed for others to be successful?

LEADERSHIP BOOKS

Once you are actively and willingly communicating, then you have to work on *how* to do it. I was telling someone what I've been up to lately, and I mentioned that I was writing this book. The person asked what it was about, and this is the sad reality of what followed.

"Well . . . let me see . . ." I said. "It's a book about . . . um . . ."

I looked up to the ceiling as if the words were suddenly going to fall from the heavens. "It's kind of like . . . you know." That was a lie—the person most certainly did not know.

I continued, "It's maybe a different style than you might be thinking." I felt like I was on a roll. It was my first complete sentence. "I find I'm bored by most books, even though there is often a great message. I'm trying to bring a solid message but be more engaging. I'm trying to be different, you know."

I saw the person nodding but looking confused. I hadn't even come close to explaining what the book was about. I tried again.

"It's a book for leaders. Like, you know, about leadership." I paused and then continued. "Yeah, leadership!"

I was somehow happy with myself for characterizing the book in the least descriptive, broadest possible sense. "It's for leaders. It's a lot about empowerment and really simplifies it." I could see the skepticism written all over the person's face. "It's about giving Context and Authority to empower someone. You'd really have to read it to understand."

At that point, I had made a total fool of myself, and the person still had no idea what I was talking about. I'm sure they wanted to say to me what people tell bad singers who want to be professional musicians: "Don't quit your day job."

BLANK STARES

Good communication is more of an art than a science. I am trying to get better at it every day, and I think every leader should do the same. How you communicate can make or break empowerment. Good communication helps people understand. If anyone on your team is doing something without understanding, you have failed.

We talked earlier about parents who don't answer kids' "why" questions. Good leaders not only answer why questions but also proactively give explanations without being asked. There won't always be time to explain complicated concepts, but you can just slot the topic into the person's training path for when there is more time.

You should continually use phrases such as, "This is why we do this." For example, "This is why this decision was made a couple of years ago," or "This is why we don't see this as an option." That understanding positions people to be empowered and to succeed on their own.

Good communicators are always on the lookout for gaps in understanding. They observe verbal cues, or they simply ask people directly whether they understand.

I often spot a lack of understanding in meetings when I see people staring blankly or when I think about what they know or don't know. In a recent meeting, the presenter gave the group an earful of acronyms and technical jargon. I asked whether anyone was actually understanding. I thought it was a rhetorical question because I was totally lost, but the room went silent. Here's the problem: Many of them weren't being honest.

I talked after the meeting with the presenter about simplifying complex concepts to make it easier for people to follow. He admitted that it was hard for him to get through the material because it was so heavy. We discussed next time asking who is able to stand up and present the same thing in their own words. And if everyone is still quiet, just pick someone randomly. (I'm kind of joking and not joking all at the same time.)

EASING INTO THE HOT TUB

Communication that empowers people is important during meetings, but it also applies to passing conversations and writing. You have to communicate in a way that gives the the audience the power to understand, and ideally contribute.

The biggest communication mistake people make is not being aware of the audience. People often only think about what they are saying, but they forget to consider to whom they are saying it to and why. Good communication requires the communicator to tailor the message for the audience and the purpose.

When telling someone about this book, I need to understand who I'm talking to and why. That should affect everything I say. If a family member who knows my personal story is curious about what I'm up to, I can just give a quick summary. If I'm talking with another

CEO, I would try to relate to his or her situation to generate interest in my book's concepts so that he or she will want to read it. I must know my audience and the reason why the information should be shared. I communicate so that the audience can understand and so that the intended purpose can be achieved. Here are a few pointers for communication.

First, ease people into the subject matter. Picture an old man getting into a hot tub. He dips his toe in, maybe even a whole foot, and then pulls it out again. Then he slowly eases his frail body into the warm water—little by little.

When you immediately unload the details of a topic on people, it's like you are throwing the old man into the hot tub. That's the mental picture I see when someone hits me with insane amounts of detail out of nowhere.

During a work day, people are thinking about many things. So, when you show up to share new information, ease them into your topic. Start broad, and then bring in details. Don't start by saying, "I was thinking about tweaking the price of the premium model version add-on from $109 to $117—what do you want to do?" Help the old man slowly get into the hot water.

(Wait a second, doesn't this make me the old man in this comparison?)

POINTLESS DETAILS

Another tip: Speak the same language. Will the people I'm talking to understand the words I'm using? Am I overcomplicating a subject? If you're overly technical while updating nontechnical people, don't tell them you're finishing committing files for patch twenty-four or that you had an idea come out of your retrospective. Speak English (or the language with which you mutually decide to communicate).

And that blends right into my last tip: Omit distractions. Choose your words carefully, and stay on topic. Don't include pointless details (like tank tops in the gym or old men in hot tubs, for example). You're trying to balance understanding and efficiency. You could tell me that you got a call from Jim last Tuesday afternoon, but does the exact day matter for what you're trying to say? What if Jim called Tuesday morning— would that change what you're about to tell me? In this example, I only need to know that Jim recommended our product to a prospective client.

These tips will help you communicate well as a leader, but you also have to help your team communicate effectively as well.

That's it for Context. Are you with me so far? Do you understand it enough to be able to teach someone else these principles? If so, let's move on from making sure everyone has Context to support the Authority that has been handed out.

SUMMARY

- Sharing Context is an ongoing process, not a one-time step.

- Maintaining Context is all about communication—making sure to communicate well.

- A leader must be on the lookout for Context gaps and to fill people in when the gaps are found.

- Leaders should consider the perspectives of others to ensure they know what they need to know.

- Advanced notice is key to helping people prepare and to participate to the fullest extent.

- Ongoing Context requires an inclusive and transparent leader; inclusive to make information widely available and transparent to share as much as possible.

- Communicate in ways that help people understand; don't just share information.

- When communicating, cater to the audience and pursue your purpose.

- You should ease people into conversations, zooming out at first before getting into details.

- Avoid pointless details in communication, such as being too technical or giving distracting information.

Ask yourself: Am I sharing everything needed for my team to be successful? How can I improve my communication?

- TWELVE -

DEFEND AUTHORITY

Let me tell you about a couple of sports I know very little about. Let's start with golf.

I played golf one time about fifteen years ago. I was the typical person who was convinced it would be easy. But that's not how it went down.

I'm not a violent person, but about twenty minutes into the experience I was ready to break my rental club on the tree that my ball could not get around. It was a weird juxtaposition of tranquil scenery and inner rage. To get even with golf, I never went back.

I'm told golf is a game of technique and intricate details. I certainly believe it now. (What I don't understand is why people stick with it.)

The second sport is swimming. My experience with professional swimming is watching the Olympics and seeing the insanely close race endings. Similar to golf, it often seems to come down to the littlest details, like how the swimmer turns around or whether he or she glides a little too long at the finish instead of squeezing in one last stroke.

It's amazing to me that the top five swimmers in the world can finish so closely together. Winning first place means sponsors, fame, and fortune. The fourth-place finisher, who is only 0.01 seconds behind is forgotten. That's only ten milliseconds, but she's seen as a nobody.

These two examples highlight the nuances and subtleties that separate the greatest athletes from everyone else. And that's how I see leaders' actions to support the Authority of their teams. The littlest detail of how a leader acts makes a massive difference in whether people keep exercising the power they have been given. But leaders rarely look closely at how their actions affect the way people own their roles, even though I would argue that it's critical for success.

LOW-HANGING FRUIT

Here's a typical conversation that I have with people who are new to taking ownership. I'll warn you in advance that it may sound like a joke. I mean, it could be funny, but it's not a joke. There *is* a difference.

Someone might come into my office and say, "What do you want to do about x?" (Note that x falls under their ownership, not mine.)

Questions like that are "low-hanging fruit" to a leader. The leader knows the answer, and it is tempting to give the answer. This is the empowering leader's age-old dilemma: to answer or not to answer. But you need to be disciplined. If you answer, you are basically an accomplice in the person's own demise. If you constantly take the low-hanging fruit, you'll end up having to pick all the fruit forevermore.

It took me a while to perfect, but my patented response to resolve the dilemma is: "What do *you* want to do about x?"

The person usually answers hesitantly, but then more confidently with each word. "Well, we could do y and then z."

"Great—let's do it!" I say.

This type of exchange will occur fifty to one hundred times, give or take, over a period of a few months. We'll call this kind of interaction phase A: *the blanket asker.* This is someone who asks you a wide-open question and expects you to come up with the entire solution.

Then over a couple of months, the conversations shift to phase B: *the specific asker.* Watch carefully for minor improvement.

People ask, "Do you want to do y?" They work their ideas into the question, but they still aren't making a decision without you.

My response is one of two, depending on my mood. If I feel polite, I ask, "Do *you* want to do y?" Or if I want to be annoying, I say, "I hear a statement disguised in that question somewhere."

They respond, "I think that's a good idea because . . ." And they go on to show they had great ideas. If I didn't ask them, I'd never know, and they wouldn't have had the chance to share their ideas or grow in confidence.

These types of interactions are great opportunities to reinforce the Authority of someone on your team. Just say, "You decide." Try it sometime, and see how the trust you give people breeds confidence of ownership.

Similar to phase A, this pattern will likely happen over a couple of months, and maybe another fifty or one hundred times. But it all becomes worth it next.

Next it's Phase C: *the suggester*. The person starts bringing suggestions. The wording will sound like this: "I suggest x, and if you are silent, I will walk out of this office and execute." It's a beautiful thing compared to where you started, but there's a little more progress to be had.

Finally, there's phase D: *the decider*. That's the goal. You want to see people making decisions based on the Authority they have been given.

You should know that people will probably work in some of phase A and B even when they've moved on to C or D. (You can just see this unpredictability as a challenge to spot and respond accordingly.)

BITE YOUR TONGUE

If you've handed Authority to a person, you need to bite your tongue. Refuse to tell people what to do or give them answers. (Note that I don't mean Context, which you can provide anytime.) They should be the ones who offer suggestions and opinions, not you. You're going to have to speak less and avoid dominating conversations.

If people come to you, get them engaged and talking. You have to draw opinions out of the owners. You need to develop what I call their "authoritative voice." It's about them gaining confidence in their Authority.

And if someone comes to you for counsel about something that falls under another person's domain, don't answer. Instead, direct that person to the owner. Validate that person's ownership.

You have to stay out of people's way and let them own their role. Be their advocate. Your subtle actions matter too. If you are not the owner of a task or meeting, don't assume even small responsibilities and limit your speaking.

Sometimes it is the most helpful leaders who are prone to accidentally taking someone's Authority. I've seen nice people with good intentions fall into controlling others even though they are simply trying to help. Too much assistance makes people feel less like owners when you're taking over all the time.

It's different if a person asks you for specific help, such as providing more Context or validating an opinion. Or, if you have a lot of margin and you want to offer someone help, it's fine to ask, providing you know that you will only be helping, and not in control.

In addition to the specific roles I've mentioned, defending Authority also applies more broadly. For example, I discussed allowing feedback and opinions from people. The leader is responsible for setting the right atmosphere where feedback is welcomed and encouraged. Many people don't naturally speak up, so you must cultivate a feedback culture.

To do this, you should ask questions and draw out responses until people see that you sincerely want the feedback. If you shut down ideas or show little interest in them, you set a negative tone. If people are fearful of sharing ideas, they will stop. You want your team members to take ownership, so it's up to you to constantly encourage them in this.

SURFING SECLUDED BEACHES

During the transfer of ownership, you should have discussed expectations. Now you need to respect them. Allow me to illustrate what I mean.

I was on vacation on a Caribbean island a long time ago, and I wanted to go surfing. There was a problem though; I had no idea where I could rent a surfboard or where there were good waves. So, I did one of the more adventurous things I've done in my life. I left my comfortable resort and walked to the busy road to flag a taxi.

When a small, dilapidated motorbike slowed down next to me, it wasn't exactly the type of taxi that I'd pictured. Then there was the language barrier. The driver spoke Spanish and no English—not "beach" and not even "hello." I'd planned ahead and learned how to say "surf" in Spanish, and that was literally all the driver needed to speed off down the road. I had no clue where we were going or how long it would take. But that wasn't my responsibility; it was his.

We ended up in the middle of nowhere about a half-hour later. We left the main road and went down a dirt road. All of a sudden, I could see a beautiful, secluded beach with one or two surfboards leaning against a straw-roofed shack. I was excited to have made it, but then I started to wonder how I was going to get home. No other taxis ever came to this place, and this was a time before cell phones. I had no backup plan.

I got off the bike and tried to ask the guy whether he could come back to get me. I tried every Spanish word I knew, all five of them. But my communication attempts failed miserably. Finally, he looked around, walked to grab a stick, and wrote "3:00?" in the sand. I nodded in agreement.

I still remember that feeling of watching him drive away. He had ownership over my transportation, and we had agreed on a time, but I didn't know this guy at all. If he bailed on me, I was in huge trouble and might never get home. I really thought I could die on that remote beach.

This story illustrates how you should deal with your team. Once expectations have been clearly agreed on, and after you have handed over a role or task, you must stay out of it. At the beach, I didn't have a choice, so it was easy for me in that situation. But it won't be as easy when you're sitting at your desk with a multitude of ways to check in on someone.

I couldn't make a call to make sure the taxi was going to be on time. I couldn't remind the driver to make sure his bike had enough gas. And I couldn't step in and drive the bike myself. It was all up to him. He had complete ownership of the end result to pick me up, and I couldn't get in the way.

Many leaders would do well to have no option to check in on people after ownership has been properly established. But in your case, it will probably take discipline. You're going to have to suppress your curiosity if you want the person to truly take ownership.

If you're frequently checking in or forcing next steps to happen, who is the owner—you or the other person? In my opinion, it's you. If you have established clear expectations, and if the person understands they can come to you if they need help, then you need to allow the person to own the role and to initiate contact when needed.

I recently had a conversation with a friend who was constantly asking for status reports from someone who reported to him. After discussing his actions, he said to me, "Man, I can't believe I'm a micromanager!" It's these subtleties that reveal who really owns the role.

WHAT-IFS

Let's cover a couple of common questions you may have about transferring ownership. First, what if there are reasons to change the expectations after they have been communicated? Obviously, that doesn't match with the taxi scenario, since I had no option for this, but it will likely happen to you. The answer is simple; you get together again with the owner and have another distinct moment to amend the expectations. For example, what if a deadline has to change? You discuss this with the owner and make sure it's feasible. And you communicate what you know about why the change needs to happen.

I'll end with a more complicated concern: What if someone fails? What if the motorcycle taxi guy had forgotten about me and there was no pick up? When you hand off ownership, there is an element of risk. You have to let people fail from time to time. After all, if they own the role, they should have the responsibility to figure out how to achieve the desired outcome. But what do you do about failure?

First, as I discussed earlier, Authority grows as trust is earned. You don't give away ownership to people working in areas where failure could cause serious problems. You certainly want to mitigate the amount of damage that can be done. (But everyone messes up sometimes, so mistakes can happen no matter how much you prepare.)

With critical deadlines, I like to agree on a due date that is well before catastrophic damage occurs. Doing that gives people on your team a clear timeframe and avoids the need for you to micromanage the work. Don't be the micromanager disguised as a nice guy who steps in to help a few hours before the deadline. Let it play out. If that time comes and goes, then it's time to address the issue.

This is where correction comes in, which happens to be a key component in reinforcing someone's Authority. We may have a consistently empowered team with Context and Authority, but there is still a role for a leader to keep people accountable and to give feedback. This may seem like an unpleasant topic, but we have to cover it. If all goes well, I'll have removed the stigma attached to correction.

SUMMARY

- Nuances can separate great leaders from others when it comes to reinforcing the Authority of others.

- The littlest details of how you act makes a huge difference in whether people keep exercising the power they have been given.

- After delegating Authority, you must refuse to instantly answer questions.

- Guide your team's progress toward taking full ownership:
    - Phase A: the blanket asker
    - Phase B: the specific asker
    - Phase C: the suggester
    - Phase D: the decider

- Saying to people on your team "you decide" shows trust and breeds confidence.

- You must develop the authoritative voice of your team by asking questions and drawing out answers and opinions.

- Being overly helpful can unintentionally take away someone's Authority

- You must maintain the shared expectations that were established when delegating Authority, including the planned outcome and timeline.

- Status check-ins should be initiated by your team.

- If the agreed upon expectations are not met by your team, instead of micromanaging, you should have a correction conversation.

Ask yourself: Do I consistently support the Authority of my team? How can I improve the way I act around them?

- THIRTEEN -

CORRECTION

When I see an issue that should be corrected, I'm tempted to ignore it and to live blissfully in denial. I tell myself it probably won't happen again.

For example, the other day one of my sons called his brother a "butt-cheek baby." (That's very, very bad when you're three.) I had a debate in my head over whether to say something, wondering what my wife had overheard from the other room. I chose to ignore the offence. My wife, who is less tolerant of inconsistent correction, nicely corrected me to pass on the correction (almost like correction dominoes).

Because of my tendency to turn a blind eye, it's critical for me to remind myself of why correction matters. I need to be certain of its purpose so that I am motivated to address each issue. If you view correction as a horrible thing, you may need to reframe your opinion.

Let's start with the word itself. Correction sounds heavy and substantial, which is not always the case. So how about we say "constructive feedback" for now?

BAD APPLES

There are a number of reasons why issues should not be ignored; I am going to address three. First, constructive feedback provides an opportunity for someone to learn and improve. In the case of my son, my wife and I believe it's better for him not to call other people names that derive from their anatomy. We give him this feedback for his benefit.

Another reason feedback matters is to preserve the culture. There needs to be consistency in how people act. You've heard the expression, "One bad apple spoils the whole bunch." I've seen a lot of companies that ignore the bad apples, and the team becomes resentful as a result. As a leader, you have to make sure you don't let things slide to the point that the desired culture is lost. Next thing you know, everyone is going around calling each other butt-cheek babies (and no one wants that).

Preserving culture is especially important with empowerment, which is more about Context than rules. Continual, open, and honest dialogue is essential. Feedback culture is what allows for a Context-based approach instead of an overload of rules and policies.

The last reason feedback matters is for leaders to maintain trust and optimism in a person for the future. I talked before about assuming success instead of failure, but neglecting issues has the effect of reverting your assumptions back to failure each time. You work hard to help someone become empowered, but if issue after issue isn't addressed, you eventually stop trusting the person with responsibility. And just like that, you're back to assuming failure and thus control.

Those are the three reasons why feedback matters: to help someone grow, to preserve culture, and to maintain optimism. Now we can talk about how it should work. Let's say you notice an issue. What do you do?

LATE-NIGHT SWIMMING

When an issue occurs, you first have a decision to make about whether it is serious enough to address. Here's the key question: Was the Context extremely clear? Was the person set up to make a sound decision?

Allow me to illustrate. I've been known to push the limits at resort pools and stay well after closing time. (I'm a rebel, I know.) There is usually a sign with rules next to the pool which includes swimming hours. The most empowering signs even describe why the hours matter, such as to keep the noise down out of respect for other guests. When it's past closing time, and a security guard comes to tell me I have to leave, I don't feel controlled. I'm disappointed, yes, and certainly embarrassed. But I understood the rules and made the decision to break them. That's on me, and I have no reason to disagree with being corrected.

In other words, I was empowered with the Context I needed. If that wasn't the case and if there were no pool rules posted, the conversation should be more about education than correction.

Let's say someone on your team misses a deadline. It might seem simple, but perhaps the Context was not provided adequately. Did the person know about the exact date? Was ownership clear? And zooming out even more, did the person know the value of excellence and reliability? The person should know that meeting deadlines matters.

You can see why controlling correction is tempting. You're annoyed the deadline was missed, and you want to blame someone. But if the Context wasn't clear—perhaps the ownership was fuzzy—guess who should take the blame? Next time you can do a better job of communicating, but this time it's your fault.

If you get mad at someone who didn't know the due date, that person will feel unbelievably deflated. The person will believe he or she is incompetent, will likely resent you and be scared of you (since you seem irrational), or be less engaged at work. You could educate the person and broader team on the value of ownership, but that is different than correction.

So, to review, if Context is unclear, we clarify. And if it was clear, we address the situation. The question is, how do we tell people to get out of the pool?

AN AFFIRMATION SANDWICH

An open and honest feedback culture should allow for real-time conversations without making a big deal about each matter. For example, let's say Sally was hosting a meeting but didn't have the room set up on time. You could say, "Hey Sally, it would be great if you could have meeting visuals pulled up before people arrive so that we make the most of our time together." That's just a quick piece of feedback that doesn't demand an official correction conversation.

The extent to which you offer minor feedback on-the-fly is subjective. I have no rules for you, but I'll tell you my thought process. I give immediate feedback for a small offense, if there's no demonstrated pattern, and if I feel I can address it in a kind way. The Sally example met all of the criteria so I would address it immediately.

As for addressing everything beyond that, I believe this should be done in a distinct moment, not at the second something happens. I used make a scene the moment I was annoyed, but I've seen since seen that as a huge failure on many levels. It's important to take the time to understand the issue and to plan how to address it in the best way that values people. However, don't wait too long; you want to address the problem while it's still fresh in your minds.

Once you take that time, some people suggest a "compliment sandwich" format. That's starting the conversation with a compliment, squeezing in the issue, and following it with another compliment. For example, you could say, "You're a swell person, your jokes aren't funny, and you have really nice socks on." That doesn't work for me. Please just tell me my jokes aren't funny (and on another day, please do still mention the socks).

The problem with compliment sandwiches is that people get used to criticism coming. They get tense when you say something nice and can see you as insincere. You don't want that affecting your role as a mentor.

Instead, I prefer an "affirmation sandwich" (please don't quote me on that wording). For example, "I really care about your success here; I would really like to see you improve at x, and I see tremendous potential in you and want to support you."

With that in mind, here is what the correction portion of the conversation looks like. You start by listening.

The temptation in these conversations is to point out everything the person is doing wrong and explaining what needs to change. Please don't do that. You have to ask the other person for his or her perspective first. Did the person notice an issue? Are there aspects he or she would do differently next time? Maybe the person is completely overwhelmed and has too much work. There are many reasons to hear someone out.

You might discover that the person already knows what you are about to say. So why not go the empowering way and let him or her say it instead of you? You might not have to address the issue if they self-diagnose and guide the conversation, which is the ideal outcome. But if this doesn't happen, we should continue with the correction process.

The next part is also about asking questions and listening, but it's a little more directed. The goal is to make sure the person had the necessary Context. Did he or she feel empowered? You could ask whether the expectations were clear enough, for example the timeline. You want to make sure the person saw a direct connection between the issue and the expectations.

Maybe you thought it was clear, but the person didn't. If the issue isn't a frequent occurrence, you'll give him or her the benefit of the doubt and not argue about it. Take note to be even clearer next time.

Now you can do some talking. You can clarify expectations for the future and explain why they matter. At this point, I recommend being direct and not talking around the issue. Speak with candor, yet still in a nice way. For example, "It is extremely important that we meet deadlines because it affects x and y, and we place tremendous value on excellence as a company." Try to connect your conversation to your values, as a point of reference. The person you're correcting should walk away having no doubt what is expected in the future.

Finally, you must decide on the next steps. Should you take any actions based on what has happened? For example, perhaps you want to give someone more training opportunities for Ability or Context. Maybe roles should be adjusted. You should make changes that reduce the chances of the problem happening again.

GOING YOUR SEPARATE WAYS

If the same issue keeps popping up for a person, you might need to go your separate ways. You know, say good-bye, call it quits. Okay, I'll just say it—you may have to consider termination.

I believe that the moment you launch an empowerment culture and clarify expectations everyone starts with a clean slate. All past wrongs are erased. But when expectations are beyond clear, issues become more significant. If the same problem happens multiple times and each instance is addressed, and if the person has received helpful mentoring, then I believe termination is the only option. You need to decide your tolerance limits when there are repeated problems. Every scenario requires discernment.

Let's say someone isn't thorough. The person might be in a role where mistakes are very costly to the organization, yet he or she is sloppy and sometimes negligent. You've discussed this two times before and tried to help, yet there continues to be a pattern of not being thorough. That for me means it won't work out.

One thing that you should keep in mind is that some people don't work well in an environment where Authority is handed over and there is little stereotypical management. Unless you are willing to invest significant time and training to help change a person, you should recognize that some people are better suited to a controlling environment.

I'll be honest: None of these things make it easier to let someone go. You can have all the greatest reasons in the world for why someone doesn't fit, but it's still hard. You walk the person through the disconnect between the intended culture and his or her actions in a caring way that values the individual. But the culture is nonnegotiable for you, and the rest of your team appreciates it, so you must maintain that.

If you have to let someone go, then you should update the team right after it happens. This Context will be important to them. Be honest, be vulnerable, and reinforce the value of the remaining team members. Use this as an opportunity to affirm people and encourage them. Maybe you'll spot people who would benefit from a one-on-one conversation. Don't ignore your team's feelings, they're important.

That's it for empowering correction. You can stop being so uptight and relax now. Now we can move on to a more pleasant topic: investing in people and taking time to mentor your team.

SUMMARY

· Many leaders naturally want to ignore issues and avoid correcting people.

· Feedback is necessary for three key reasons:

 · Provides an opportunity for growth as a form of mentoring.

 · Preserves the desired culture, especially since empowerment culture is more about Context than rules.

 · Maintains trust and optimism in your team.

· When deciding whether to address an issue, ask if the Context was clear, and if the person was set up to make a sound decision.

· It is extremely deflating to be corrected for something you couldn't have known about.

· If the Context was unclear, you should clarify the matter with the person and resolve to do better next time; but if the Context was clear, the issue should be addressed.

· An open and honest feedback culture should allow for real-time conversations done in a kind way, especially for small, simple offenses with no ongoing pattern.

- For everything else, you should quickly address matters in a distinct moment while the topic is fresh, but with enough time to be intentional about your response.

- Be sure to affirm the value of people and make sure that they know that you care about their progression (no compliment sandwiches).

- Be sure to listen first during correction conversations, seeking his or her perspective and making sure Context was clear.

- Expectations should be clarified during correction conversations to set the Context for the future.

- Next steps with correction could include training opportunities, adjusting roles, or even termination if a repeated pattern continues.

Ask yourself: Do I provide feedback often enough when issues come up? How can I improve with the way I give feedback and correction?

- FOURTEEN -

INVEST IN OTHERS

I recently had supper with a friend; a guy I've known for a long time who is ambitious and successful.

I tend to skip past small talk with people, and this meal was no exception. My first question was something along the lines of, "Are you actually happy these days?"

He went on to tell me how overwhelmed he was with life. He had climbed the professional ladder and had a significant position—way ahead of people his age. But a lot of his work was not his passion. To make things worse, his manager was pushing him to do more of the same: keep growing his skills, take extra projects, and so on. At first, he referred to this guy as a mentor.

I asked him, "Why don't you just talk to him about how you're feeling? Share what's really going on."

His reaction was emphatic, as if I'd just asked him why he didn't start flapping his arms and fly away from the table, which would have been an equally ridiculous question. "Oh, he wouldn't hear me out for a second!" my friend replied. "He shuts down this type of conversation. He avoids problems and pretends everything is great. He'll interrupt me and say, 'Keep your head up,' or something useless like that. He just wants me to keep moving in the direction I'm heading and doesn't want to hear anything else."

I asked, in a confused tone, "So he has no clue how you're feeling and isn't interested in talking about it?"

"Exactly," he said.

"I've got news for you, dude. He's no mentor."

BLISSFULLY UNAWARE

This story illustrates two issues. The first is how someone who is supposed to be a mentor can be oblivious to how people are truly doing. His manager was totally disconnected from my friend's real feelings and state of mind.

Have you ever spent time with someone who you hoped would help you in some way, but you left dejected because he or she wasn't attentive to your situation? In your mind, you were practically waving an SOS flag, but the person was oblivious. Maybe you were discouraged, overwhelmed, bored, or unhappy, but the other person had no idea what was going on with you. If you reported to that person, then you could feel unseen or lost, as if you were at a masquerade party and no one saw the real you walking around.

When someone lacks awareness of your needs, it can make you feel used, which blends into issue number two. This one's a little subtler, but it's a big one for me. I believe the primary motivation of a mentor makes a big difference in how the relationship plays out.

Managers, like the one my buddy had, are first driven by their own benefit or gain. They approach you only to get something. That's when you feel used.

I know people who leave me feeling that way. I'm suspicious when I see them calling. I'd almost rather they stopped being fake and just said, "I want to take advantage of your generosity and use you for something that helps me." Okay, thank you for the honesty! Now I can help with your request, and have it be more of a transaction. I guess people could also do better at faking their real intent, but I don't think someone could get that by me.

In my friend's case, he did benefit from being challenged to do positive things, such as to improve his skills. But it was ultimately connected to his manager's master plan.

My friend's manager was concerned about the task, not the person. The manager invested in my friend for what he could get out of him. And I think people notice selfish intent, even if they realize the benefit as a by-product. People know when they're being sold to or used.

You could empower people, but they could be doing amazing work while not loving it. If you don't pay attention to their well-being, they'll reach their limits of being used and probably leave.

On the other hand, real leaders are first driven by the benefits they give to others (which usually helps the leader too). The leader is aware of what is going on and acts on what he or she is hearing. Good leaders want to add value to people and enrich their lives through the work they are doing. They are interested in not only the task, but also in seeing people grow and be positively impacted. You want the work people do to align with their passion and pursuits.

INVESTING WISELY

The drive toward business excellence and accomplishment can feel at odds with valuing people first. In my experience, it seems to be more common to see the work coming before the well-being of people. I've spoken to people who believe it's nonnegotiable to compromise on excellence. But somehow they think it's fine to overwork or control their team. That's weird to me, and shortsighted, but it happens every day.

For example, what if a project is behind schedule, and there is a firm deadline for the final product that can only be made by significant overtime and personal sacrifice? Can people still be the first priority?

I've heard of companies giving their staff unlimited energy drinks. This sounds thoughtful and kind, right? Not exactly. It's basically poison for your body, and for one main purpose: so people can work inhumane hours to make crazy deadlines. It's completely self-serving for the company, but it's disguised as a perk. That's not putting people first.

Even if there is a temporary strain on someone, there are still ways to put them first. You can ask to help out or offer resources, or you can show you appreciate the effort, or try to get the due date changed. Whatever the case, you won't let the pressure continue long term.

You want a team that takes on ownership and is engaged for the long haul. That means you'll have to care enough to invest in people and help them thrive. When you care about people, you create an environment where people want to be empowered and to do their best work. You can empower people and see some success, but it will be short-lived if you don't value them. Empowerment can't be seen as a means to an end with people being used to accomplish a result.

The ultimate challenge to your commitment to being a mentor comes when you help someone grow, only to see the person leave for somewhere else. But if you really care about a person, you have to be okay with that person potentially moving on.

This chapter is about investing in your team, and you can do that for your benefit or theirs (or somewhere in between). I will, however, be focusing on the latter: investment primarily for the benefit of others. This type of investment includes being aware of others and then acting on that awareness to add value. You typically reap the benefits, too, but really it's just the right thing to do.

WALK WITH ME

I recently spoke with a CEO of a rapidly growing billion-dollar company. (Sounds impressive, right? Sadly, you'll be less impressed when you hear the Context.) I haven't seen a lot of people doing what I'm proposing in this chapter, so when I heard a prominent leader talk about some of this stuff at a conference, I had to stalk, I mean talk, to him.

The CEO, who will remain nameless, briefly mentioned something in his keynote session that got my attention. He said that he spends a lot of his time talking to his key leaders with almost no agenda. He asks them how things are going, how he can help, and what obstacles might be in the way. When I heard that, I needed to know more.

I strategically found a spot he'd have to pass on his way out of the building, and I cut him off. He debated talking to me for a couple of seconds, probably feeling overwhelmed from speaking and having a mob of people meet him as he walked off the stage. In a matter-of-fact tone he said, "Walk with me," and he started walking out of the building.

I quickly asked him more about how he organized his time. I wanted to know what exactly he did each day. (I know, it sounds a little creepy, given the stalking and all.) He said his time was divided evenly between three things: holding individual meetings with the key five to ten people who report to him, mingling with teams to see how he could help with important projects, and doing normal CEO things. So, over 66 percent of his time was spent with people, which is interesting given the fact that he's a self-proclaimed introvert.

Remember that being a leader is a role, not a title. And the role is investing in people. Any time someone is doing this, I believe they are being a leader. Here's a big shocker: To invest in people, you have to *be* with actual people every now and again. That's exactly what this guy did.

This is tough for introverts like me and my CEO friend. (That's right, a three-minute walk and a similar disposition and I'm calling him a friend.) You can't hide away in your office all day and call that leadership.

Ironically, the greatest distraction I've recently had from investing in people has been writing about investing in people. I am naturally drawn to working independently, so I have to force myself to walk around, get some fresh air, and be with people.

PERCEPTION

Becoming aware of how people are doing is a tricky thing. Knowing the condition of your team is not like other metrics on a dashboard. It would be cool to have alerts that show when someone needs a conversation, or needs to be appreciated, or is overwhelmed. But that's not how it works.

I know a guy who is legendary at reading people. One quick look at your face, and he'll know something is off. He has a constant pulse on the people around him. Some people are gifted at this, and have a high level of emotional intelligence, which is important to develop as a leader.

However, if you don't feel gifted in the area of perception, all hope is not lost. I fall somewhere in the middle. I spot a lot of things and wonder how others don't see them, but I can also miss some signals. (I can almost hear my wife shouting "Amen!" as I type this.) I have to make a conscious decision to think and engage like a mentor since it doesn't always come naturally.

I certainly want to keep improving in this area, so I try to interact with people to monitor how things are going for them. For example, I'll join a meeting and notice someone who doesn't seem to be participating or passionate about the topic. Or I'll hear a subtle reference to someone being lost or overwhelmed. I won't ignore any of those things. You can see why margin is crucial.

I try to keep a regular rhythm of one-on-ones with key staff. When we sit down, I am direct and ask deep, open-ended questions. Deep questions lead to substance, which requires probing to get beneath the surface. In business, this means fewer questions about the details of tasks and more discussion about vision, values, growth, and feelings.

For those who are closed off, this can be a little uncomfortable. However, I find that most people welcome having someone care enough to ask meaningful questions. Experiment sometime and see how it goes. Ask your flight attendant what the toughest part of his or her job is. Or ask a friend about the most challenging thing he or she is dealing with.

Open-ended questions aren't overly framed. I've had conversations with people during which the other person tried hard to ask deep questions, but the questions were too specific. As a result, limits were placed on the answers and they lacked depth.

For example, let's say I wanted to ask how you felt about the chapter on insecurity. An overly framed question could look something like this: "Do you feel insecure when someone else on your team does something impressive, such as making a big sale, and everyone notices their work, or are you more insecure when you aren't the center of attention in a meeting?"

That leaves almost no space to maneuver. When you focus on specific points, you limit the person's choices to one or two answers, even if neither is applicable. Moreover, the question is long, which is always a failure for me. (If you need to use three commas in a question, it's probably too long. Can we make that a rule?)

Asking open-ended questions can also mean removing bias and having less of an agenda. For example, you could ask someone, "Was it insecurity that held you back from publicly congratulating the people on your team for the great work they did?" Obviously, that's a leading question. It's more of a statement that prevents you from getting to the heart of the matter.

Instead, you can open up the questions by asking something like this: "Do you ever feel insecure as a leader?" Then go from there. It's more empowering to give the person something to work with, through a question that's not overly framed. Keep in mind that the question is the Context from which someone will draw his or her response. I said before that good communication is more of an art than a science, and this is especially true when asking deep, open questions.

Here are some examples of questions you could ask your team:

- How are you feeling?
- How is it really going?
- Are there any barriers I can help remove?
- Can I help with anything?

- Is anything defeating or bothering you?
- Are you overwhelmed?
- Are you challenged enough?
- Are you enjoying what you're doing?
- Do you find your job fulfilling?
- Do you think you're excelling at your work?
- Are there areas in which you lack confidence?
- Are you growing in your role?
- Are you withholding feedback or opinions?

These examples demonstrate the idea, I hope. Please don't write this list on cue cards and spout them off next time you talk to someone. Questions should be tailored to the person and situation. A person's response should affect the path you take with follow-up questions.

ONE-SIDED CONVERSATIONS

This might sound obvious but asking questions isn't enough—you also have to listen to what they're saying. You may need to ask more questions initially with people to draw out feedback, problems, and honest thoughts; but once they know you offer a safe space, they'll get used to engaging. It's far more important for leaders to listen than to talk.

When I see a doctor, there's usually only one person listening, and it's not him. The doctor gives me time to say about fifteen to twenty words max, and then it's all him. (The last time I saw my doctor, I started with a sarcastic joke, and I'm pretty sure he deducted those words from my quota.) When the word limit is reached, the doctor interrupts and tells me what to do. The solution often addresses a symptom, but not the root issue. It's a bandage. The doctor is not fully empowered with Context, so I don't feel good about the exchange.

By contrast, have you ever been in a conversation with someone who made you feel you mattered to him or her? Maybe the person listened intently and wasn't distracted. Perhaps the person helped you make sense of your world. That is the goal.

Attentiveness should not only make the person you're with feel better, but it also gives you a deeper understanding. You look for clues in what people are saying and consider actions you should take. You primarily monitor intangible things, like feelings, so you'll really have to pay attention. With this understanding, you are empowered to take action.

Sometimes, a person needs a little encouragement. Maybe he or she is in a new role and is nervous about using certain skills. Sincere encouragement could really help with confidence.

People also need to know that you appreciate them and the contributions they make. Appreciation isn't always with words; for some it could be training opportunities, new equipment, or (the classic) money.

You may notice an adjustment is needed. A person could have too much work, in which case you could pull in resources to help. Or maybe someone's career path should change. You could help him or her make that transition.

Next I will address how to take action to help a person grow. This is the mentor-investor role.

MAXIMIZING POTENTIAL

What are you doing now to help people grow? Good mentors should know how well each person on their team is growing in relation to where each person could be. Based on that awareness, you have an active role to do whatever you can to help people progress. You keep an eye out for potential growth and partnering opportunities that could help them realize that potential.

Mentors help to increase the areas in which a person is empowered, which brings us back to Ability, Context, and Authority. We previously covered how to establish these three elements in the "Empower" section, but I want to focus now on growing these components, using similar principles.

Earlier, when I wrote about how to empower people, I mentioned the importance of making sure a person has the skills to do a certain role. But a mentor takes a more holistic approach. What other skills do people have that they aren't using? You want to maximize each person's Ability.

For example, you might notice that someone on your team is friendly, so you think of the various areas where he could be empowered to use that Ability. A friendly person may be in customer support, but maybe he is pulled in for certain sales presentations to use his skill there. Are you leveraging all the skills that each person has?

With Ability, you maximize what a person has and you think about improving skills. Solving one shortcoming could unlock a whole new area of contribution for someone. You can spot these things and be a champion for getting help. For example, maybe someone is decent at critical thinking, but there would be so much more value if they were proficient at it. You can provide that person with opportunities to learn from others, to practice and improve.

You can also focus on expanding the Context of the people around you. Small gaps in Context could have a big impact in the types of roles a person can take on. For example, a salesperson could learn more about finances to be able to create proposals.

I now find myself constantly thinking about expanding people's knowledge and understanding. It's always on my mind and integrated into the way I operate. I almost never take phone calls without someone else in the room who is getting a chance to learn more. When I'm in meetings, I often take time during or afterward to provide extra background information that helps set people up for increased success in the future.

Finally, you should be intentional about growing the Authority of the people on your team. Are there people who are close to being able to take on more responsibility? What can you do to help? For example, you might know someone wants to do sales demos. Why not give him or her chances to speak on a less critical demo? I believe in giving people opportunities that challenge them.

Again, it's up to leaders to partner with their teams to help them grow. But we have to make sure each person owns his or her own development. You are helping people, but ownership ultimately must rest with each person. Good mentors eventually work themselves out of a job.

It's taken the whole book to get to the point of being positioned for growth, which may have been your primary motivation to learn about empowerment at all. Let's wrap up with that in the conclusion.

SUMMARY

- Empowerment can't be seen as a means to an end with people being used to accomplish a result.

- The primary motivation of a mentor should be to benefit others.

- The people on your team should be better off because of you and the work they do (which usually helps you and the organization).

- Leaders must sincerely value people.

- Investing in people requires intentionally spending a significant amount of time with people.

- You must be fully aware of what is going on with each person on your team.

- Regular one-on-one conversations should happen with the people on your team.

- You can set the tone of conversations by not talking about tasks and instead asking deep, open-ended questions and then listening.

- Questions could include: How are you feeling? Can I help with anything? Are you overwhelmed?

- Pay attention for ways to appreciate people for their efforts, to maximize strengths, or to spot opportunities for growth.

- Help people grow by training, sharing more Context, and expanding Authority

Ask yourself: What am I doing right now to help the people on my team grow? How can I make a greater investment in people?

CONCLUSION

I had a brilliant idea for how to end this book. I thought about tracking down Captain Tank after all these years to see how he's doing. It would be a nice link back to the introduction.

Maybe he found someone who helped him figure out his technique, and now he's massive. We'd have a good laugh about the bicep-kissing story. It would be a great time.

Or what if he was the same old guy who was still struggling at the gym every day and not seeing results? I'd introduce myself and show him the way, while applying the techniques in this book. He'd become an incredible success story to share with the world. Next thing you'd know, he'd be in the Olympics for weightlifting and teaching other people how the right form makes all the difference. He'd always wear an *Empower Then Lead* shirt (it would be a tank top, of course) and share his success story with the world.

What a conclusion that would have been! So inspirational. So symmetrical.

SCALING THE MOUNTAIN

The story of Captain Tank illustrates how leaders need to do the right things to make more impact. I made the case for a two-phase framework to outline what you should do: First empower your team, and then be an others-focused leader. Stated differently, you'll pursue empowerment over control and leadership over management.

Everything starts with seeing people's potential and assuming they will succeed. You'll then set people up to be empowered so you're not involved in the details. This is all a setup phase. You can't skip it or rush it. If you want to set yourself up for the long term, you can't cut corners in the short term.

To then be a leader, you need confident humility to focus on elevating others. You need margin and to be less busy, allowing you to go back and empower more people. Then you'll be the biggest advocate for culture. You'll be deliberate to do whatever encourages your team to remain empowered. Lastly, you'll invest in others.

Then, and only then, you will be positioned for growth and advancement. You can expand and not burn yourself out. This growth can partially start the empowerment cycle again—you empower more people while continuing to lead. In a sense, the process described in this book is empower, then lead, then empower, then lead, then . . . You get the idea. With each new plateau of growth, you repeat the process. It's like mountain climbing: You make some progress and then stop to catch your breath before you continue upward to the summit.

You will also grow more leaders, so that eventually you will just be leading other leaders. You will keep pushing Authority deeper into the organization. Your impact will go from *what* you can directly affect to *who* you can empower and release.

Those are the right things to do if you want growth with less direct involvement. That was my goal as I transitioned to empowering leadership. Maybe the desire to see this type of expansion is what drove you to read this book. You've trudged through the pages only to find the part you most care about is in the conclusion. Nevertheless, you can dust off your vision binders and pursue what's in them, like advancement and expansion. The difference now is that the growth will last and be sustainable.

Those points are all the benefits that you might see in the marketing material for this book. They will encourage people to give these concepts a shot. They might compel people to consider the empowering approach, if their lives are out of control. I could end the book here, but I want to share more details about my personal experiences and be completely transparent about my transition to empowerment.

WARMED NUTS

When I hit a wall in my business, I was desperate to expand but I was so involved in the day-to-day tasks that I couldn't move forward. I finally realized that I was the bottleneck preventing growth.

Someone I respected told me to take a step back for a few weeks during the summer and just read. That was his professional opinion—to read. To me it sounded like a prison sentence, not because I dislike reading, but because it meant pausing my life. Nevertheless I read books like my job depended on it. I didn't read a single one about empowerment, but it was the uniform theme that I perceived to be woven throughout.

I became convinced empowerment was the solution, so I gave everything I had to implement this new way of life. I committed 100 percent.

I spent the next twelve months mainly in the implementation phase. I took every role I owned and transferred it to others. My New Year's resolution was to do absolutely nothing myself. (I liked how dramatic that phrase sounded and the reactions it got from people when I shared it.)

I obsessed over seeing my team thrive because I saw potential benefits for me. I focused on expanding Context for people and giving them opportunities to see what they were capable of. I was consumed with this empowerment initiative, and it was the driving force behind most of what I did. But what happened next was something I didn't foresee.

Have you ever been on a road trip during which you enjoyed the journey so much that you were surprised when you arrived at the destination? I remember the first time I flew in first class. (As if one story wasn't enough, now I'm telling a story within a story.)

It was a multi-hour flight, but it felt like minutes. What stood out to me the most wasn't the free food and drinks, or the hot towel that was literally presented on a silver platter. It was the warmed nuts. I'd never had warmed nuts before (insert joke here). I didn't even know there was such a thing.

I got seconds, but the guy traveling with me didn't. Then he realized he'd made a big mistake when mine came, and he asked for more. The flight attendant had more nuts, but they weren't warm. They were room temperature. He went from not knowing warmed nuts existed to being disappointed he'd be eating normal room-temperature nuts.

I digress, but my point is that the empowerment phase was for me like that first-class flight—I was caught off guard when the wheels touched down.

At first, the idea of developing an empowered team seemed like a lot of work. I messed up all the time and couldn't see the end in sight. But then out of nowhere, I was there. It crept up on me.

I suddenly realized that my team had become very comfortable in their areas of ownership. They consistently made great decisions without me. I was minimally involved and only at the right times. I also had a great group of people who were moving into leadership roles, taking even more responsibility away from me. The demands on me reduced significantly. I found myself with a lot of time on my hands to use as I wanted. The business was incredibly stable, almost running itself. And it was expanding, all while not depending on me.

This all started with a change of leadership style, from controlling to empowering. (Don't get me wrong; I'm still on a journey and mess up sometimes, but the way I lead is night-and-day different than before.)

A strange thing happened for me during this year-long phase. I grew to love the journey of seeing the dramatic changes in people's lives as they became empowered. It was thrilling to be part of such a turnaround. I saw people who had hated coming to work come alive. People were thriving, with the results transferring into their personal lives.

SELECTIVE FULFILLMENT

I can now finally put words to my experience. I went from being obsessed with achievement to caring about fulfillment. Achievement is generally selfishly motivated and it doesn't make a person happy in the long term. Fulfillment, on the other hand, is about others.

I should have seen the light sooner. At times I was a workaholic control-freak wanting to close the next big deal. But I also had this inner longing to help people in less fortunate areas of the world. Let me sum up: I'd achieve what I could *at* work and then have a rare fulfilling moment *outside of* work. Let me explain what I mean by this.

I fought this dichotomy for years, especially after I went to a remote area of Kenya about a decade ago. There was a serious drought, and lives were in danger. The cause was exactly in line with my passion, and I wanted to help. My company was able to send a bunch of food, and I was able to fly there to see it being distributed firsthand. I flew on a tiny four-seater plane to a dirt landing strip in the middle of nowhere, and an entire village gathered to meet me as I touched down. I was twenty-four years old.

Perhaps the most fulfilling moment of my life to date happened on that trip. There were hundreds of people lining the hills as far as the eye could see, just waiting to be called to come up and get a bag of food to take back to their mud huts. While the people were waiting, someone got me to stand up so the people could thank me for the food. It was an overwhelming feeling.

That moment cemented my feelings about the value of humility. I couldn't believe those people who had so little from a material point of view were thanking me, who had so much. Wasn't helping them just my responsibility as a fellow human being?

Then I left Africa and went back to work. The fulfilling moment ended, and I went back to pursuing achievement with minimal care for people. Do you see the disconnect? I was living a life of extremes between achievement and fulfillment. I was like a pendulum swinging from micromanager to humanitarian-aid philanthropist, with nothing in between.

My empowerment journey showed me a connection between leadership and fulfillment for the first time in my life. Leadership didn't have to be about achievement first; it could be about fulfillment as well. I also learned that I could enjoy focusing on other people instead of myself. Achieving more growth and expansion was superficial, like building big biceps. It looks good, but what's the point? I found out I wanted something more than that.

TRUE IMPACT

I used to define "impact" as making more money and growing something, but now I see it as influence in the lives people. Positively affecting people is now what impact means to me. (And, incidentally, that seems to help you achieve in the process.) Everyone knows that doing something for people is more fulfilling than doing something for yourself. But that truth is rarely lived out in the business world, and even more rarely applied to leadership.

There are some famous CEOs who people can't stand to be around. Is that really success? Is that the dream? I remember hearing an interview with a guy who was close to one of these CEOs, and I was disgusted. This was a guy many people idolized and put on a pedestal. He may have had great ideas, but he was not a great leader. He was certainly brilliant, but he was a jerk. He was a brilliant jerk.

Ask yourself what you want from your life. Do you want to build an organization and make increasing amounts of money? Or do you want to lead other people and make a positive impact in their lives? Setting other people up for success is rewarding leadership, where fulfillment comes from focusing on others first.

Are you ready to make other people the heroes? Are you ready to set other people up for success and to help them reach the potential they are capable of? Will you choose to empower instead of control, to lead instead of manage? Do you want to build a legacy that lasts beyond you?

Whether or not this occurs is entirely your choice. You're empowered now but it's up to you to take the first step.

SUMMARY

- *Empower Then Lead* two-phase framework summary: Empower your team and then be an others-focused leader.
- You can always improve in pursuing empowerment over control, and leadership over management.
- With true leadership and an empowered team, you are positioned for growth and advancement.
- In reality, you will go back and forth between the empower phase and lead phase as you continue to grow.
- A sign of healthy, sustainable growth is when you empower leaders that empower other leaders.
- Authority should keep moving deeper into the organization.
- Your potential impact shifts from what you can directly affect to whom you can empower and release.
- Leadership doesn't have to be about achievement first, but fulfillment.
- This framework allows for a bigger impact, but true impact becomes about positively affecting people.

- Setting other people up for success is rewarding leadership, where fulfillment comes from focusing on others first.

Ask yourself: Am I fulfilled as a leader? What is the impact I seek to make? Where will I start in progressing toward my goal?

AFTERWORD

I don't know when to stop, do I? I'll be even more transparent now. This might start sounding like a diary, but if you've stuck with me up to this point, you must be down for anything.

I've recently hit an impasse in my life. I have loved seeing my team become empowered, but now I want to do more. The extra time I have on my hands has been a blessing and a curse. With options, people become pickier and they get to choose where they spend their time. I want to help other leaders discover the fulfillment that comes from empowering people and embracing the role of a leader. I don't know exactly where this will take me, but I want to spread this message.

I'm not saying this is the path your life will take—moving from your business to inspiring others. (I don't want too much competition in this fulfilling leadership space; that would cut into my achievement.) Regardless of where you land, I hope you can grow, expand, and free up your time. But I hope most of all that your team will experience the benefits of empowerment and that you will realize fulfillment in what you do.

I suppose this book is my resignation letter in a sense (albeit a little long-winded). I no longer want to be exclusively dedicated to the software business, as my passion is stronger for sharing this message.

I wasn't sure if I should be this transparent about my journey, but I wanted to be honest about the outcome and to share this Context with you. I got what I wanted, but then I wanted something else.

As I write this, I'm imagining a scene from a long TV series that ends with the main character walking off into the sunset and into the unknown. Where one journey wraps up, another begins. Thanks for coming along with me.

Matt

Finished reading Empower Then Lead? We would love to hear from you! Please visit www.EmpowerThenLead.com to leave any comments, questions and feedback you have.